The relationship of Christ and the church is not like a marriage – it is a marriage! Consequently, any picture of healthy marital dynamics will also point our hearts to the Gospel itself. Solomon's great song is an inspired glimpse that allows us to look beyond that marriage to the great marriage. Down through the centuries many have read The Song and reflected deeply and devotionally on Christ and the Church. This collection contains some genuine Gospel gold. Let these writings not only push you into the biblical text, but may they push you prayerfully closer to our wonderful bridegroom too!

PETER MEAD
Director of Cor Deo;
Author, *Lost in Wonder: A Biblical Introduction to God's Great Marriage*

The history of biblical interpretation is a rich resource of Christian devotion and theology alike. Earlier generations of Christians knew that the Song of Songs is less about romantic love or erotic poetry than it is spiritual fidelity. Tim Chester has compiled a treasure trove of writings on the 'most biblical' of all the books in Scripture, so called because of what it is ultimately about: God's love for his people; Christ's love for the church; the love of the saved for the savior.

KEVIN J. VANHOOZER
Research Professor of Systematic Theology,
Trinity Evangelical Divinity School, Deerfield, Illinois

"The Song of Songs is one of the most exposited books in church history, and Tim Chester helps us see the ways its verses have been interpreted. In dozens of devotional entries, Tim delves into the writings of Gregory of Nyssa and Charles Spurgeon, Martin Luther and J. C. Ryle, Ambrose and Matthew Henry, as well as many others, to help us think about Solomon's most famous Song with the cloud of witnesses who have gone before us. An enriching and fascinating read!"

MITCHELL L. CHASE
Preaching Pastor, Kosmosdale Baptist Church, Louisville, Kentucky; Associate Professor of Biblical Studies at the Southern Baptist Theological Seminary, Louisville, Kentucky; Author, *Short of Glory*

In the last two centuries of modern biblical criticism, the Song of Songs has been interpreted as ancient love poetry and nothing more, which is a radical departure from premodern biblical interpretation. Even conservative historical criticism has put up little resistance to this rejection of the unified premodern tradition. But this book is one of the many encouraging signs of change. It is odd that Evangelicalism, with its emphasis on piety and revival, should have adopted an interpretation of the Song which obscures its stress on the longing of the soul for God. This book takes us back to the beautiful and tender tradition of the classical, Christological interpretation, which makes the modern interpretation seem shallow and boring. Highly recommended!

CRAIG CARTER
Research Professor of Theology, Tyndale University, Toronto, Ontario; Theologian in Residence, Westney Heights Baptist Church, Ajax, Ontario

MEETING CHRIST IN THE GARDEN

A DEVOTIONAL OF CLASSIC WRITINGS ON THE

SONG OF SONGS

TIM CHESTER

CHRISTIAN
FOCUS

Copyright © Tim Chester 2023

hardback ISBN 978-1-5271-1015-1
ebook ISBN 978-1-5271-1072-4

10 9 8 7 6 5 4 3 2 1

Published in 2023
by
Christian Focus Publications Ltd,
Geanies House, Fearn, Ross-shire,
IV20 1TW, Great Britain.

www.christianfocus.com

Cover design by
Catriona Mackenzie

Printed and bound by
Bell & Bain, Glasgow

Contents

Foreword

When did you last hear a sermon series on the Song of Songs? Perhaps you're now smiling wryly because your church is going through the Song right now. But it's not common, and that's revealing. At one level, it simply tells us that Song of Songs is often thought of as a niche book about the sensitive subject of romantic love and sexuality. Yet perhaps our neglect of the Song reveals something deeper and more concerning. Today, Christians commonly bemoan the spiritual shallowness and lovelessness they see in the church, and rightly so. We see too much mechanical religion, fuelled by duty, expectation, and even fear, rather than delight in Christ. Is there a connection to our neglect of the Song of Songs? I think so, for the Song gives us a spiritual tonic that we have clearly not fully taken.

As this book so beautifully shows, the Song of Songs is a holy of holies, taking us deep into the innermost reality of Christ's burning love and compassion for His people. By so doing, it inflames our love for Him, and stirs in us as we read it a heartfelt enjoyment of God. That is why you should read this wonder-filled collection of writings, and let them lead you deeper into the Song: they will make you yearn for more fellowship with such a lovely Saviour. Use it as a daily devotional or gobble it up in chunks, for here is medicine for the heart that tastes like the sweetest strawberries.

Michael Reeves
President and Professor of Theology
Union School of Theology
Wales

Introduction

The great nineteenth-century preacher Charles Spurgeon described the Song of Solomon as the Most Holy Place. He compared the historical books of the Bible to the outer courts of the temple, and the Gospels, Epistles, and Psalms to the Holy Place: the place that only the priests could enter. His point was that, to a greater and lesser extent, all these books bring us near to God. But the Song of Songs is *the Most Holy Place*, the inner sanctum, a holy of holies. It 'occupies a sacred enclosure into which none may enter unprepared.' That's because in the Song we meet Christ. The garden portrayed in the Song is a location created in the imagination, in which we may spend time with Christ and enjoy His love. The language of human love is intended to evoke an experience of divine love, and inspire in us a response of love. The Song channels our desires towards their true end, our Creator and Redeemer.

Throughout most of the history of the church, the Song of Songs has been seen as a picture of God's love for His people and Christ's love for His church. Some commentators focused on the relationship between God and the individual soul; others saw the Bride in the Song as the church as a whole. But all agreed the Song used the language of human love and marriage (perhaps a specific marriage of King Solomon) to evoke God's love. Only in the nineteenth century did scholars start to regard it primarily or exclusively as a celebration of human sexuality. This view dominated the scholarship of the twentieth century. But there are signs the tide is turning again back to the classic view.

Read in the light of the wider Bible story, it is hard to avoid the allusions to God's relationship with His people. So many other passages speak of God's love in marital terms or liken our infidelity to adultery (Exod. 34:15; Ps. 45; Isa. 54:5, 62:5; Hosea 1-3; Ezek. 16; Jer. 11:15, 12:7; Eph. 5:22-32; Rev. 19:6-9).

But there are also indications within the Song itself that it's intended to picture God's relationship with His people. Some descriptions of the woman seem more like descriptions of a landscape. She is likened to the land of Israel because she represents Israel. The woman also comes to her wedding out of the wilderness in a column of smoke (Song 3:6, 8:5), just as the people of Israel came to covenant with God at Mount Sinai out of the wilderness, led by the pillars of cloud and fire. Moreover, the poem is full of garden imagery that takes us back to Eden – the place where God walked with humanity. The tabernacle and temple were also full of garden imagery. Written into the architecture of the temple was the promise of a restored Eden. And that promise is also written into the poetry of the Song. No wonder Spurgeon thought of it as the Most Holy Place.

In this book I've drawn from the rich history of reflection on the Song of Songs. I've lightly edited the extracts, mainly by replacing archaic words and shortening sentences. I've used an ellipsis (...) to indicate where I've removed larger sections, but, to avoid cluttering the text, I've not used one where I've merely left out a few words or sentences.

More or less every verse of the Song is covered to provide a good introduction to the Song. And included are contributions from commentaries/reflections from the fourth to the nineteenth centuries to give readers a good feel for how Christians have traditionally read the Song. But my main aim has been to provide a collection of devotional treasures that point us to the love of Christ. My goal is that we might draw near to God through the Song.

A number of extracts make connections between the exalted language of the Song and our everyday experience in a way that enables us to put it into practice. But, in many ways, I think the primary aim of the Song is to *inspire* us not to settle for a half-hearted sense of Christ, but to pursue Him more – to know His love not just in theory, but in our own experience. If that's something you want, then read on!

As we prepare to enter the holy territory mapped out in the Song, let's join with the twelfth-century Benedictine abbot William of St. Thierry in this prayer.

> As we approach ... the marriage song,
> the song of the Bridegroom and the Bride,
> to read and to weigh your work,
> we call upon you, O Spirit of holiness.
> We want you to fill us with your love, O Love,
> so that we may understand love's song –
> so that we too may be made in some degree participants
> in the dialogue of the holy Bridegroom and the Bride;
> and so that what we read about
> may come to pass within us.
> For where it is a question of the soul's affections,
> one does not easily understand what is said
> unless one is touched by similar feelings.
> Turn us then to yourself,
> O holy Spirit, holy Paraclete, holy Comforter;
> comfort the poverty of our solitude,
> which seeks no solace apart from you;
> illuminate and enliven the desire of the suppliant,
> that it may become delight.
> Come, that we may love in truth,
> that whatever we think or say
> may proceed out of the fount of your love.
> Let the Song of your love be so read by us
> that it may set fire to love itself within us;
> and let love itself be for us
> the interpreter of your Song.

1.

Gregory the Great on the Song of Songs 1:1

The Song of Songs, which is Solomon's.

Our experience of earthly desire is designed to enflame our longing for God. Gregory the Great says this is what the Song of Songs does for us if we read it aright: it uses the language of human love to ignite our passion for God. Gregory (c. 540-604) was an early pope, the first from a monastic background. He was the pope who first sent missionaries to southern England.

In the Song of Songs, the language of what appears to be physical love is employed that the soul may be revived from her numbing cold by means of her usual manner of speech, so that she may grow warm again and so be spurred on to the love that is above by the language of the love here below. Now in this book there is mention of kisses, there is mention of breasts, there is mention of cheeks, there is mention of thighs. We should not ridicule the sacred narrative for using such language. Rather, let us ponder how great God's mercy is. For when he mentions the parts of the body and thereby summons us to love, note how wonderfully and mercifully he works within us. He has gone so far as to embrace the language of our vulgar love in order to enkindle our heart with a yearning for that sacred love. Yet God lifts us by understanding to the place from where he lowers himself by speaking. For we learn from dialogues of the love here below with what intensity we should burn in the love of Divinity.

Let us consider this book carefully lest we linger over exterior meanings when we hear the words of exterior love. Otherwise the very crane employed to lift us will instead burden us and thus not lift us. In these bodily words, in these exterior words, let us seek whatever is interior. And when we discuss the body, let us become as if separated from the body. Let us attend this sacred wedding of the Bride and Bridegroom with an understanding of the most interior kind of charity, which is to say, with a wedding gown. Such attire is necessary since if we are not dressed in a wedding gown, that is, if we do not have a worthy understanding of charity, then we will be cast out of this wedding banquet into the exterior darkness, which is to say, into the blindness of ignorance.

By means of this passionate dialogue let us cross over to the virtue of impassibility. For just as Sacred Scripture consists of words and its meaning, so too a picture consists of colours and its subject matter. And he is dumber than dumb who pays such close attention to the colours of the picture that he ignores the subject depicted! So if we embrace the words expressed in an exterior way and ignore their meaning, it is as if we were ignoring the subject depicted by concentrating only upon the colours.

- Think about your own experience of love, whether that is one of joy, frustration, or pain. How does this point to God's love for you?

2.

Richard Sibbes on the Song of Songs 1:1

The Song of Songs, which is Solomon's.

Richard Sibbes describes how Christ came in human flesh so that He might be our bride, and the Holy Spirit comes to persuade us to consent to the marriage. In this marriage we not only receive Christ, but all that belongs to Christ. Sibbes (1577-1635) was a leading Puritan preacher and theologian.

The Holy Spirit is pleased here to condescend to our weaknesses. That we might help ourselves in our spiritual state by our bodies, he speaks here of heavenly things after an earthly manner, and with a comforting mystery. As in other places the Holy Spirit sets out the joys of heaven as a sweet banquet, so here he sets out the union that we have with Christ by comparing it to the union of the husband with the wife. That we might better understand what this union is, he condescends to our weakness, that we might see that in a mirror what we through our corruptions could not otherwise discern. This book is nothing other than a plain demonstration and setting forth of the love of Christ to his church, and of the love of the church to Christ. The Holy Spirit is pleased by bodily things to set out these spiritual things, which are of a higher nature, so that by thinking and tasting of the one we might be stirred up to translate our affections (which in youthful age are most strong) from the heat of natural love to spiritual things, to the things of God. All those who are spiritually-minded (for whom chiefly the Scriptures were written) will take special comfort and instruction in this way ...

There is a civil contract between a husband and wife which firmly resembles the spiritual contract between Christ and his church.

That this civil contract may hold, both parties must consent. So it is between Christ and his spouse. He was so in love with humanity, that he has taken our nature upon him; and thus his incarnation is the ground of all our union with Christ. His incarnation is the cause of our union with him in grace here, and our union in grace is the ground of our union in glory. Now, that we may be a spouse to him, he gives us his Spirit to testify his love to us that we might give our consent to him again and also that we might be made into a suitable spouse for him.

Likewise in marriage there is a sharing of all good things. So it is here. Christ here in this spiritual contract gives himself, and with himself all good things. His Spirit is the church's. His happiness is the church's. His graces are the church's. His righteousness is the church's. In a word, all his privileges and prerogatives are the church's. As the apostle says, 'All things are yours, and you are Christ's' (1 Cor. 3:21-23), for all are Christ's, and all that are Christ's are yours by this spiritual contract (Hos. 2:19-20).

But what have we to bestow upon him in return? Nothing at all; neither beauty nor riches, nothing except our miserable and base condition that he took upon him.

This is a well-spring of much comfort, and a ground of much duty. Christ, who has all things, condescended so far down to us, to take us to be his spouse. What then can we lack when we are connected to the fountain of all things? We cannot want any protection, for that is covered in this well. We cannot want any good thing, for he will supply what we need. We have free access to him, just as the wife has to her husband.

- Think about what belongs to Christ that now belongs to you because you are part of His bride.

18

3.

Teresa of Avila on the Song of Songs 1:2

Let him kiss me with the kisses of his mouth!
For your love is better than wine;

We would never have the temerity to ask to be kissed by God, says Teresa of Avila, if God Himself did not encourage us to do so in the Song of Songs. Teresa sees the kiss as a sense of God's peace, a peace which give us the courage to serve God in a hostile world. Teresa (1515-1582) was a Spanish mystic and reformer within the Carmelite monastic order.

'Let him kiss me with the kisses of his mouth.' O my Lord and my God! What words for a creature to utter to its Creator! Blessed are you for having taught us in so many different ways! Who, O my King, who would dare to speak in this way without your permission? It is astounding! ... Yet the soul inflamed and intoxicated with love cares for no other meaning, and only desires to utter these words, since you do not deprive us of this privilege. God help me! Why should we be so amazed? Is not the reality still more wonderful? Do we not draw close to you in the most blessed sacrament? ...

For if, my Lord, a kiss signifies peace, why should not souls ask this of you? What more can we beg of you than what I plead for now, O my Master, that you would kiss me with the kiss of your mouth? ...

O holy Bride! Let us ponder the kiss for you, which is that sacred peace with God that encourages the soul to wage war with worldliness, while remaining perfectly confident and calm within itself. Happy are those who enjoy this grace! It consists in such a close union with God's will that God and the soul are no longer divided, but their will is one — not in words and wishes only, but in deeds as well. When the Bride sees that she can serve the Bridegroom better in any way, so ardent are her love and desire that she disregards any difficulties raised by her mind nor does she listen to the fears which her mind suggests. Instead, she allows faith to act, seeking no profit or comfort of her own, having learnt at last that her welfare consists entirely in this conformity to God's will ...

One speech of this sort should be enough to make us belong completely to you. Blessed be you, O Lord, for nothing is lacking on your part! In how many ways, and by how many means, do you show your love! By your works, by your bitter death, by the tortures and insults you bore, by the pardon you grant us. And it is not just these acts alone that communicate your love, but the words you speak and teach us to speak in this Song of Songs. These words so pierce the soul that loves you, that I do not know how the soul could endure them were it not for the fact that you give us your help, not according to our merits, but according to our needs. I ask, then, O Lord, no more of you in this life except that you 'kiss me with the kiss of your mouth' in such a way that, even if I wished, I could not separate myself from union and friendship with you. Grant that my will may be subject to you, and may never swerve from your will. May nothing prevent my truly declaring: O my God and my glory, 'your love is better than wine' (1:2).

- Ask God for a felt sense of His presence in your life today.

4.

Hudson Taylor on the Song of Songs 1:2

Let him kiss me with the kisses of his mouth!
For your love is better than wine;

Hudson Taylor wrote a series of articles on the Song of Songs, which were later published under the title *Union and Communion*. He believed Christians often fall short of an experience of God that could be theirs, because they are unwilling to surrender themselves wholly to God. Taylor (1832-1905) was a pioneer missionary to China and the founder of the China Inland Mission (now the Overseas Missionary Fellowship).

This recorded experience gives, as it were, a divine warrant for the desire for manifestations of his presence which we can sense – an experience of his love. It was not always so with her. Once she was content with his absence – other society and other occupations sufficed her. But now it can never be so again. The world can never be to her what it once was. The betrothed bride has learnt to love her Lord, and no other company than his can satisfy her ... Now her joy in him is a heaven below.

But again she is longing, and longing in vain, for his presence. Like the ever-changing tide, her experience is ebbing and flowing. It may even be that unrest is the rule, satisfaction the exception. Is there no help for this? Must it always continue so? Can he have created these unquenchable longings only to tantalize them? Strange indeed it would be if this were the case!

Yet are there not many of the Lord's people whose habitual experience corresponds with hers? They know not the rest, the

21

joy, of abiding in Christ. And they know not how to attain to it, nor why it is not theirs. Are there not many who look back to the delightful times of their first betrothals, who, so far from finding richer inheritance in Christ than they then had, are conscious they have lost their first love? ... Others, who may not have lost their first love, may yet be feeling that the occasional interruptions to communion are becoming more and more unbearable, as the world becomes less and he becomes more. His absence is an ever-increasing distress. 'Oh that I knew where I might find him!' 'Let him kiss me with the kisses of his mouth! For your love is better than wine.' 'Would that his love were strong and constant like mine, and that he never withdrew the light of his countenance!'

Poor mistaken one! There is a love far stronger than yours waiting, longing for satisfaction. The Bridegroom is waiting for you all the time. The conditions that prevent his approach are all of your own making. Take the right place before him, and he will be most ready, most glad, to satisfy your deepest longings, and to supply your every need ...

Could there be a sadder proof of the extent and reality of the Fall than the deep-seated distrust of our loving Lord and Master which makes us hesitate to give ourselves entirely up to him, which fears that he might require something beyond our powers, or call for something that we should find it hard to give or to do? The real secret of an unsatisfied life lies too often in an unsurrendered will. And yet how foolish, as well as how wrong, this is! Do we fancy that we are wiser than he? Or that our love for ourselves is more tender and strong than his? Or that we know ourselves better than he does? How our distrust must grieve and wound afresh the tender heart of him who was for us the Man of Sorrows! What would be the feelings of an earthly bridegroom if he discovered that his bride-to-be was dreading to marry him, lest, when he had the power, he should render her life insupportable? Yet how many of the Lord's redeemed ones treat him just like this! No wonder they are neither happy nor satisfied! ...

Our attention is here drawn to a danger which is pre-eminently one of this day: the intense activity of our times may lead to zeal in service, but to the neglect of personal communion with Christ. But such neglect will not only lessen the value of the service, but tend to incapacitate us for the highest service. If we are watchful over the souls of others, and neglect our own souls ... we shall often be disappointed with our powerlessness to help our brothers and sisters ... Let us never forget that what we are is more important than what we do. All fruit borne when not abiding in Christ must be fruit of the flesh, and not of the Spirit.

- Is there an aspect of your life that you are not surrendering to God?

5.

Bernard of Clairvaux on the Song of Songs 1:2

Let him kiss me with the kisses of his mouth!
For your love is better than wine;

Bernard of Clairvaux sees the 'kiss' as a picture of the incarnation in which God and humanity are joined together, just as a kiss unites two people. Bernard (1090-1153) was a reforming Cistercian abbot whose spiritual writings were much prized by the Protestant Reformers. His (incomplete) sermons on the Song of Songs were first delivered to his monks.

'Let him kiss me with the kisses of his mouth.' For his teaching shall become in me a fountain of water springing up into eternal life (John 4:14). His living and powerful word is to me like a kiss (Heb. 4:12). And it is not the mere meeting of the lips (which can be a deceptive sign of peace in the heart), but rather the imparting of joys, the revealing of hidden things, and a certain, wonderful, intimate, ineffable mingling of the heavenly light which enlightens the soul, and the soul which is enlightened by it. For the one who is joined to the Lord is 'one spirit with him' (1 Cor. 6:17) ...

I do not presume to be kissed with his physical mouth. *To communicate happiness in this way is the unique prerogative of the Man whom the Word assumed to himself in the incarnation.* My petition is more humble: to be kissed by the kisses or words of his mouth - a privilege shared by all who can say, 'from his fullness we have all received' (John 1:16).

Notice, it is the Word which became incarnate who is the mouth who gives the kiss, and it is the human nature which is assumed that receives it. The kiss, in which the giver and receiver are one, is the one Person constituted of both divine and human natures, the mediator between God and men, the Man Christ Jesus (1 Tim. 2:5) ...

What a happy sign, and what wonderful condescension, in which, not lip is pressed to lip, but God is united to humanity. In a physical kiss the pressure of lips signifies the union of souls. But here a union of natures joins that which is divine and that which is human, and so reconciles things on earth with those in heaven. For he is our peace, who has made the two one (Eph. 2:14). It was for this that every ancient saint longed, because they felt the assurance beforehand that upon them his joy and gladness would be abundantly poured, and in him were hid all the treasures of wisdom and knowledge (Col. 2:3). And so they longed to receive his grace and his fulness (John 1:16) ...

Moreover, we must add that he who declares himself to be our mediator before God is the Son of God, is God himself (1 Tim. 2:5). 'O LORD, what is man that you regard him?' (Ps. 144:3) What confidence allows me to trust myself to such great majesty? How can I, who am but dust and ashes, presume to think that God would take care for me? Between him and his Father is perfect love. So he has no need of me, nor of my possessions. How then can I be sure that my mediator will be faithful to me? Yet if God has truly determined, as you say, to have mercy on me, and meditates great acts of grace towards me, let him make a covenant of peace, let him make an eternal alliance with me (Isa. 61:8), sealed by this kiss of his mouth. In order that the words of his lips should prove effective, let him empty himself, let him humble himself, let him stoop from his high heaven (Phil. 2:7), and kiss me with the kiss of his mouth. Let the Son of God, if he will be a mediator acceptable to both parties, and suspected by neither, become human, become the Son of Man, and so establish my trust on a solid foundation.

When I perceive that the Son of God is also a son of my own human race then with assured confidence shall I take him as my mediator. I can no longer harbour any suspicion of him, since he is my brother and my flesh. For my hope is that he will not be able to despise me, since he is bone of my bones, and flesh of my flesh.

- Praise God that, by being connected to Christ by faith, we are connected to God.

6.

Ralph Robinson on the Song of Songs 1:3

Your anointing oils are fragrant;
your name is oil poured out;
therefore virgins love you.

Ralph Robinson links the 'anointing oils' in the Song of Songs to the anointing of Jesus by the Holy Spirit. This anointing instils a beautiful fragrance into the life, death, ongoing intercession, and words of Jesus. Robinson (1614-1655) was a Puritan preacher in London, who remained loyal to the monarchy.

The Scripture mentions Christ being anointed with the graces of the Spirit as our Mediator. This ointment was shed upon the Lord Jesus in such great plenty that he may well be called by the name 'ointment' (Ps. 45:7) ... The Spirit was not given him by measure, but beyond measure (John 3:34). He was from his conception filled with the Holy Spirit. He was full of grace and truth (John 1:14). He had not only drops, but whole rivers of oil poured upon his head. His Godhead anointed his manhood with an unspeakable fulness (Col. 1:19) ...

Ointment is fragrant and yields a very sweet smell. And the Lord Jesus Christ is very fragrant. He is sweet in himself, and he is exceedingly sweet in the nostrils of his saints. The perfume described in the Law was a picture of him (Exod. 30:34). He perfumes all persons and places wherever he comes. If there is one drop of Christ poured upon the soul, the whole soul is perfumed with the smell of it ...

There is a fragrance in his person. He is a bundle of myrrh (Song 1:13). His life and holy conversion gave out a sweet smell in the world (Ps. 45:8). The grace of the Spirit (of which his life was full), his righteousness, meekness, piety, patience – what a smell they cast abroad in the gospel to this very day.

There is a fragrance in his death. His death was a sweet savour unto God (Eph. 5:2). His dead body was embalmed with sweet spices (John 19:39), not that he had need of this for his body never saw corruption (Ps. 16:10). So fragrant was the death of Christ that he has perfumed the grave, and made it like a bed of roses for all the saints.

There is a sweet fragrance in his intercession. The intercession of Christ is so sweet that it perfumes heaven itself (Lev. 16:12-13). The odours of the sweetest incense are not so fragrant to the nostrils of people, as the odours of Christ's intercession are to God. So fragrant is his intercession that the services of his people, which are unsavoury in themselves, come up as a cloud of incense before the Lord ... All this sweetness in the church and in her services is because they are perfumed with the incense of Christ's mediation ...

There is a fragrance in the word of Christ. The breath of Christ's mouth is sweeter than any perfume in the world. This is what the Church mentions in Song of Songs 5:16: 'His mouth is most sweet.' All his promises and precepts are very savoury. There is a fragrance in all his ordinances. Prayer, sacraments, preaching, singing of Psalms are in themselves, and to a gracious heart, like a sweet-smelling ointment. The church mentions this in Song of Songs 2:3: 'his fruit was sweet to my taste.' There is no sweeter air that blows under heaven as the fragrance in the church of God where the ordinances of Christ are dispensed in power and purity.

In summary, there is nothing of Christ that is not more sweet than the best ointment that ever was compounded by humanity.

- Today, some of your actions may not please God, but Christ's intercession on your behalf means you yourself always bring God pleasure.

7.

Charles Spurgeon on the Song of Songs 1:4

Draw me after you; let us run.
The king has brought me into his chambers.
We will exult and rejoice in you;
we will extol your love more than wine;
rightly do they love you.

Charles H. Spurgeon, who himself struggled with depression, invites us to counter negative thoughts and distractions by affirming the truth to our own hearts. Spurgeon was a noted intercessor, but he also recognises here the value of silence before God. Spurgeon (1834-1892) was perhaps the greatest English preacher of the nineteenth century. In addition to preaching regularly to thousands of people, he founded an orphanage and a ministry training college.

Of course, in prayer and in praise, we speak to God. But I suggest that we should seek to have much more of intense and familiar intercourse with the Lord Jesus Christ than most of us at present enjoy. I find it good sometimes in prayer to say nothing, but to sit or kneel quite still, and to look up to my Lord in adoring silence. And then sometimes to talk to him, not asking anything of him, but just speaking familiarly with Jesus, realising him to be present. And waiting to hear him speak until some precious word of his from Scripture comes into my soul as with living accents newly-spoken by those dear lips which are as lilies dropping sweet-smelling myrrh ...

You will notice that we have here *a double resolve*: 'We *will* exult and rejoice in you, we *will* extol your love more than wine.' There are so many things that try to come in between our souls and our Saviour, so many sorrows that would prevent our rejoicing in him, so we must be resolved to be glad in him whatever our sorrows may be. Down with you, sorrows! Down with you! We have said to the Lord that we will exult and rejoice in him, and we mean to prove our words to be true. Then there are so many troubling thoughts that come flying in to mar our full fellowship with our Lord. However tightly windows may be closed, and doors shut, these thoughts will find a way in, and we remember the sick child at home, or some care that has afflicted us during the week. Oh, but Lord, we will not remember these things now! We say to you from our hearts, 'We *will* – we *will* – we *will* remember your love.' Away with you, care, sorrow, grief, away with you! Come to me, O Holy Spirit, and help me now to have a happy time, to exult and rejoice in my Lord – and to have a holy time to remember his love, and to remember nothing beside!

You must will it most intensely, dear friends, or it will not come to pass. It is not sufficient merely to walk into a place of worship, and put ourselves into a posture of devotion, and then imagine that, doing whatever is proper to the place and the hour, we shall have fellowship with Jesus. Oh no, beloved; oh no! We must worship him in spirit and in truth, not in fiction and in sham; not mechanically, as though we could have true fellowship with him without earnest and intense desire. No, there must be these two utterances of our holy resolve: 'We will exult and rejoice in you; we will extol your love more than wine.'

- Repeat the phrase, 'I will extol your love more than wine,' emphasising a different word each time.

8.

Gregory of Nyssa on the Song of Songs 1:5-6

I am very dark, but lovely,
O daughters of Jerusalem,
like the tents of Kedar,
like the curtains of Solomon.
Do not gaze at me because I am dark,
because the sun has looked upon me.
My mother's sons were angry with me;
they made me keeper of the vineyards,
but my own vineyard I have not kept!

Like the bride, Christians are 'dark, but lovely' – darkened by sin, but made lovely by Christ – as Gregory of Nyssa reminds us. Gregory (c. 335-395) was Bishop of Nyssa, one of the great theologians of the eastern church, and a leading defender of orthodox trinitarian doctrine.

It seems to me that the great Paul, in his letter to the Romans, makes much of a thought that is very close to this. There he establishes the love of God for us on the ground that, when we were sinners and *dark,* God made us full of light and lovely by shining upon us with his grace (cf. Rom. 5:6-8). For just as at night everything, bright though it be by nature, shares the [dark] look of the dominant darkness, but once the light comes, there remains no trace of darkness in things that had before been obscured by the night, just so when the soul has been transposed from error to truth, the dark form of her life is transformed into radiant beauty.

Paul ... says to Timothy the same thing that the Bride says to her maidens. He says that he, who earlier was a blasphemer and a persecutor and a man of pride and a dark one (cf. 1 Tim. 1:13), was deemed worthy of beauty; and further that Christ came into the world to make dark ones bright (cf. 1 Tim. 1:15), not calling the righteous to himself but calling sinners to repentance (cf. Matt. 9:13), whom he caused to shine like stars by the laver [washing] of rebirth (cf. Tit. 3:5) when he had washed off their dark appearance with water ...

And so it is that here the Bride, by manifesting the goodness of the Bridegroom, encourages the daughters of Jerusalem, saying that even if he were to take in a dark soul he would render it beautiful by its communion with him, even if some soul were a *tent of Kedar*, it would become the habitation of the light of the true Solomon – that is, of the peaceable King who has come to dwell within it. That is why she says, '*I am dark and beautiful, O daughters of Jerusalem*, in order that, looking to me, you too may become *curtains of Solomon*, though you are *tents of Kedar.*'

- Look back and gives thanks for the ways in which Christ is making you beautiful.

9.

Nilus of Ancyra on the Song of Songs 1:7-8

She: *Tell me, you whom my soul loves,*
where you pasture your flock,
where you make it lie down at noon;
for why should I be like one who veils herself
beside the flocks of your companions?
He: *If you do not know,*
O most beautiful among women,
follow in the tracks of the flock,
and pasture your young goats
beside the shepherds' tents.

Nilus of Ancyra says desire is a beautiful thing because it motivates us to seek God. And one way we see God is as His image in us is restored. The more we become like God, the more we display the goodness of God to one another. In this extract Nilus imagines the Word of God, Jesus, speaking to us. Nilus (d. 430) was a monk on Mount Sinai.

'Desire' – says [the Word] – 'is a beautiful thing, but its purpose is frustrated by reason of its still being lowly, childlike, and modest. For one cannot grasp God from the orderly way in which he governs the cosmos, but rather from the soul's purity, since in its own nature it possesses an imitation of my nature, its character of being "after the image" (Gen. 1:26). Once you have the image purified of any wicked defilement, you have me in your sights when you look upon yourself; for by every excellence that you bring to fulfilment, you are copying my nature.

'If you have not yet been able to see in this fashion and have not known yourself in your own beauty, *go out in the footsteps of the flocks,* which is to say, "make your way by following the traces of the things which I have created, and which now rejoice in my providential care," and by this searching you will see me as Creator. For just as the feet of the flock, making tracks in the earth, guide the one who is following them to the place where the shepherd is (for it is essential that the shepherd be with the flock, if it is not to be uncared for and unsupervised, deprived of a good guide) – in exactly the same way a well-directed search among created beings leads to discernment and knowledge of the Creator, to the extent that it affords a conjectural picture of what he is. In just this way David, taking the creation to be a book for contemplation, fixes his mind – a mind more than usually adapted to knowledge and science – upon created things; and looking into the reason that informs them as if it were a text to be read, he said, "I will ponder all your work" (Ps. 77:12) ...

'But she who imitates me in her own love of humanity, and in her own justice reproduces mine accurately, will no longer contemplate me by way of conjecture but clearly, because she has become by imitation what I am by nature. For to those who desire to know me I have said, "Be merciful, even as your heavenly Father is merciful" (Luke 6:36), and "Be compassionate like your Father" (Eph. 4:32), and above all "be perfect, as your heavenly Father is perfect" (Matt. 5:48). If then you do not already know yourself to be that sort of person, you will not know me either; but you will know yourself when you have been formed by the aforesaid virtues after my likeness.

'Since, however, as it seems, you are not yet able to know yourself, you should have sought me, not among the flocks, but among the saints, for I am the "Most High who takes my rest among the saints" (Isa. 57:15). *Go out in the footsteps of the flocks, and pasture your goats by the shepherds' tents,* tracking the nature of the things that are by practicing intellectual discernment, and restraining the disorderly motions of the soul by your practice.

For once you have in this way cleansed the divine image of all its defilements, it is by reference to that image – and rightly so – that you shall know me as God; for every image is naturally adapted to make its archetype known.'

- Can you think of ways in which you see something of Christ in the lives of other Christians?

10.

Alexander Moody Stuart on the Song of Songs 1:9-11

I compare you, my love,
to a mare among Pharaoh's chariots.
Your cheeks are lovely with ornaments,
your neck with strings of jewels.
We will make for you ornaments of gold,
studded with silver.

Alexander Moody Stuart applies this description of the beloved to the church. In so doing, he urges us to pursue Christ with fervour and urgency – whether around the communion table, in our Sunday gatherings, or in private prayer. Moody Stuart (1809-1898) was a minister in the Free Church of Scotland.

Having traced the footsteps of the flock ... she finds herself in his presence, seated with him 'at his table' (verse 12). The sacramental table it may be, or the house of prayer, or the closet, or 'the solitary place'. The Bridegroom first accosts her, 'my love,' responding to her own address, 'You whom my soul loves' ...

'I compare you, my love, to a mare among Pharaoh's chariots.' He compares her in this way, first, because the church, the one bride of Christ, consists of an exceeding great company. The comparison may be taken next of the conquering power of the chariot host. But especially the comparison to the chariots of Pharaoh refers to their swiftness. Christ yields to the prayer of the soul that cleaves to him in faith and love; and commends the ardour, the swiftness, and the perseverance of her pursuit ...

Longing soul, go and do likewise, and you shall be upheld by the same almighty arm, arrive at the same result of holy rest, and receive the same divine commendation ... Fear not, for he who compares you to Pharaoh's chariots does in the very utterance make you such as he calls you. It is the King's word, not only of acknowledgment, but also of command; of comparison but also of creation. And since it proceeds from his lips, and is received by faith, you are already transformed into 'the chariots of Pharaoh' ...

'Your cheeks are lovely with ornaments, your neck with strings of jewels.' You poor slave-girl, your cheeks were burned and darkened by the midday sun ... But they are beautiful now through your Saviour's beauty put upon you. Your bread was eaten with the sweat of your brow, but your Lord has wiped the tears from your eyes, and the sweat-drops from your forehead, and has adorned your brows with radiant rows of jewels. Your neck was scarred with the iron yoke, but now that neck is loosed from its bonds, and encircled with chains of gold, with ornaments of grace. They are the free gifts of your Redeemer who has delivered you ...

'Ornaments of gold, studded with silver' means either the royal or nuptial crown. Bride of the Lamb, you made for him a crown of thorns, its ruby studs were the drops of his own blood, and behold, this is the exchange he makes with you! The crown had fallen from your head, your gold had become dim, and his own diadem of beauty, his own fire-tried gold, his own crown of righteousness, he puts upon you. This crown you have in possession, though concealed beneath your soldier's helmet. And you have a yet more glorious crown promised to you when the battle has been fought and won. 'Be faithful unto death, and I will give you the crown of life' (Rev. 2:10).

- Is there an urgency to your pursuit of fellowship with Christ?

11.

Samuel Rutherford on the Song of Songs 1:12-13

While the king was on his couch,
my nard gave forth its fragrance.
My beloved is to me a sachet of myrrh
that lies between my breasts.

Samuel Rutherford says the most important thing in life is to become engaged to (to 'tryst' with) Christ. He uses the language of the Song of Songs to praise the ravishing beauty of Christ. Rutherford (c. 1600-1661) was a Presbyterian pastor and theologian. During the turmoil of the seventeenth century he was, at times, banned from preaching. So instead he wrote letters, which ever since have been prized for their Christ-centred passion.

You came to this life about a necessary and weighty business, to tryst with Christ concerning your precious soul, and its eternal salvation. This is the most necessary business you have in this life; and your other concerns beside this are but toys, feathers, dreams, and fancies. This is in the greatest haste, and should be done first. Means are used in the gospel to draw on a meeting between Christ and you. If you neglect your part of it, it is as if you would tear up the contract before Christ's eyes, and give up the match, that there may be no more communing about that business. I know that other lovers beside Christ are pursuing you, and your soul has many wooers. But I pray you to make a chaste virgin of your soul, and let it love but one. Most worthy is Christ alone of all your soul's love, even if your love were higher than the heaven, and deeper than the lowest of this earth, and broader than this world. Many, alas, too many, make a common strumpet of their soul for every lover that comes to the house. Marriage with Christ would put your love and your heart out of the eye of all other unlawful suitors; and then you have a ready answer for all others, 'I am already promised away to Christ; the match is concluded, my soul has a husband already, and it cannot have two husbands.'

O if the world did but know *what a smell the ointments of Christ cast*, and *how ravishing his beauty is* (even the beauty of *the fairest of the sons of men*), and how sweet and powerful his voice is, the voice of that one Well-beloved! Certainly, where Christ comes, he runs away with the soul's love, so that it cannot be commanded. I would far rather look but through the hole of Christ's door to see but the one half of his fairest and most comely face (for he looks like heaven!), than enjoy the flower, the bloom, and the chief excellence of the glory and riches of ten worlds.

Lord, send me, for my part, just the meanest share of Christ that can be given to any of the dwellers in the New Jerusalem. But I know my Lord is no miser. He can, and it becomes him well, to give more than my narrow soul can receive. If there were ten thousand, thousand millions of worlds, and as many heavens full of men and angels, Christ would not be pinched to supply all our wants, and to fill us all. Christ is a well of life; but who knoweth how deep it is to the bottom?

This soul of ours has love, and cannot but love some fair one. And O, *what a fair One*, what an only One, what an excellent, lovely, ravishing One, is Jesus! Put the beauty of ten thousand, thousand worlds of paradises, like the garden of Eden in one; put all trees, all flowers, all smells, all colours, all tastes, all joys, all sweetness, all loveliness, in one: O, what a fair and excellent thing would that be! And yet it would be less to that *fair and dearest Well-beloved*, Christ, than one drop of rain to the whole seas, rivers, lakes, and fountains of ten thousand earths. O, but

Christ is heaven's wonder, and earth's wonder! What marvel that his bride says, 'He is altogether lovely!' (Song 5:16).

- Is there something tempting you away from allegiance to Christ, to which you need to say, 'I am already promised away to Christ'?

12.

Ralph Robinson on the Song of Songs 1:13-14

My beloved is to me a sachet of myrrh
that lies between my breasts.
My beloved is to me a cluster of henna blossoms
in the vineyards of Engedi.

Ralph Robinson (see #6) says the beloved (i.e. Christ) is like myrrh in that, when He is close, He perfumes, preserves, and beautifies what is around Him.

The expression is taken from the practice of virgins who used to carry flowers or pomanders in their bosom. Jesus Christ is the church's pomander. He is her sweet bag which she resolves to wear continually about her, which she purposes to keep continually about her breasts ...

Myrrh has a perfuming quality, and Jesus Christ has a perfuming virtue. See how the Church describes him for his fragrance. His human nature is richly perfumed with the graces of the Spirit, and he is able to perfume all places and persons wherever he comes. The soul, that is like a dunghill, full of unsavoury and loathsome smells, is by the communication of the graces of Christ rendered marvellous sweet ...

Myrrh also has a preserving quality. It keeps things from corruption. It is used for the embalming of dead bodies, that they may be preserved from rotting (John 19:39-40). And the Lord Jesus Christ has a preserving power. He keeps the soul from rotting. Sin is a corrosive thing. In a short time it would totally putrefy the soul if Jesus Christ were not to dry up its corruption. Sin is called in Scripture a leprosy, a spiritual gangrene, a putrefying fire (Isa. 1:6). If Jesus were not every day to drop this spiritual myrrh upon the heart, the heart would soon be turned rotten. Grace would rot and moulder to nothing if Christ did not daily apply himself.

Finally, myrrh has a beautifying quality. Sin makes the soul full of wrinkles and ill-favoured. But Jesus Christ, by anointing it with the myrrh of his saving graces, removes this ugliness, and puts a bright hue upon the soul. 'Your beauty ... was perfect through the splendour that I had bestowed on you, declares the Lord GOD' (Ezek. 16:14). All the spiritual beauty of the soul is from Jesus Christ. He changes the sooty discoloured appearance of the soul into a shining beauty ...

All you that love sweet perfumes, fall in love with Jesus Christ. A soul without Christ is unsavoury. Many are much affected with sweet-smelling things, flowers, spices, and powders. Much vanity is shown in the use of these things. But get this myrrh into your bosom, and you will be perfumed in the nostrils of God. Nothing that is in you, nothing that comes from you, will have a good favour in the nostrils of God if this myrrh is not dropped upon it. Get your beds, your garments, your houses perfumed with this myrrh, and then God will love your company.

- Think about the different rooms in your house and the activities they represent – the living room, dining room, bedroom, office, and kitchen. Is each one perfumed with the fragrance of Christ?

13.

James Durham on the Song of Songs 1:15-16

He: *Behold, you are beautiful, my love;*
behold, you are beautiful;
your eyes are doves.
She: *Behold, you are beautiful,*
my beloved, truly delightful.

James Durham says that, while our *experience* of God's love often comes in response to our love for Him, we only ever love God because He first loved us. Our love is like the light of the moon, while Christ's love is like the sun whose light the moon reflects. Durham (1622-1658) was a Scottish soldier turned minister. His published works include *Christ Crucified* on Isaiah 53 and *Clavis Cantici* on the Song of Songs.

Our Lord Jesus considers it good sometimes to intimate his love to believers, and to let them know what he thinks of them. He does this that the believer may be confirmed in the faith of his love. For this is both profitable, and also comforting and refreshing. From the connexion, observe, that there is no time when Christ more readily manifests and intimates his love to believers than when their love is most warm to him. In the former verse, she has provided space between her breasts for him, and in these words our Lord comes with a refreshing greeting to her. For, although his love goes before ours as its source, yet he has ordered things so, that the intimation of his love to us, should be after the stirring of our love towards him (John 14:21) ...

She responds in the same way to him, because the same things that are commendable in her are infinitely and much more commendable in him. That which is in the believer is like an extract with Christ being the original source, and the graces that are in the believer are but the transcript or copy. All these things are in Christ like the light in the sun, and in the believer like the light of the moon, which is communicated to it by the sun. They are in Christ as in their own element and ocean, and in the believer like some little stream flowing from that infinite fountain. It's on this basis that the same commendation given by Christ to her is returned by her to him. It's as if she said to him, 'My beloved, what is my fairness? It's you who are fair. I am not worthy to be reckoned fair, the commendation belongs to you, you are worthy of it.' And this is the nature of love in believers, to blush (as it were) when Christ commends them, and to cast all such commendations back upon him, that they may rest upon Christ, as the party who deserves them best ... It is to show from where all her beauty was derived: it was from his. 'If I be fair,' she says, 'it is because you are fair. It's your beauty that puts beauty upon me.'

- Our love is 'like some little stream flowing from that infinite fountain' of Christ's love.

14.

George Burrowes on the Song of Songs 1:16-17

Our couch is green;
the beams of our house are cedar;
our rafters are pine.

In this verse, the lovers are nestled in a natural shelter formed by trees. George Burrowes see this as a picture of the shelter provided by Christ Himself, especially His divine nature. Burrowes (1811-1894) was Professor of Languages at Lafayette College, Easton, Pennsylvania.

Our place of repose is not open to the rays of the sun, nor to the rain, but is protected by a shelter, a roof with rafters of cedar, and a ceiling of fir or cypress, adorned with exquisite carved work. These were materials used in the temple; in their nature rich and enduring ...

This protection is nothing less than the divine nature of Jesus Christ. Nothing can harm us beneath this heavenly shade. Evil, Satan, affliction, death, the chill dews of sin, cannot strike us there. In the cloud lowering with wrath over our guilty world, the angel of death, the minister of divine justice, has his stand. But from his arrows of death, our pardoned spirits are more secure than she who reposed with the beloved beneath this ceiling was from the withering rays of the sun. In this overshadowing defence of the divine nature of Jesus are all the excellences of the Godhead. The arch spread over us at midnight, with its stars, nebulae, and constellations does not present to the eye, assisted by the best telescope, anything comparable with the overshadowing divinity of Christ. Like the roof, it is our shelter. Like the evening sky, it sheds dew on the thirsting soul, refreshing airs on the fainting heart, guiding light on the bewildered spirit. It reveals to our enraptured contemplation, transcendent and inexhaustible glories. God inhabited the pillars of cloud and fire that protected the camp of Israel, and at the same time communed with them through the form of a man supposed to be seen between the cherubim. So the divine nature of Christ is our glorious covering, while at the same time he in whom dwells all the fulness of the Godhead bodily communes with us through the human nature of Jesus Christ ...

This shelter can never decay. He is the same yesterday, today, and forever. We may wander to the edge of creation without being beyond the limit of this defence. The palaces of earth are crumbling, ... the temple of Solomon, with its marble, cedar, and gold, is in the dust. But this spiritual shelter of the soul, erected for us by the tree of life in the paradise of God, stands, and shall stand, through ages of ages, pure, fresh, and without decay. And when the heavens have passed away, and the earth be consumed, this refuge, the place of repose of the Beloved and his redeemed, shall emerge from the ruins, towering on the Rock of Ages in imposing grandeur, and crowned with that cloud of glory.

- Whether you feel the accusations of Satan, the threats of people, or the weight of sin, see yourself nestled within the protection of Christ.

15.

Martin Luther on the Song of Songs 2:1

I am a rose of Sharon,
a lily of the valleys.

Having warned us not to start trusting in our own righteousness
again, Martin Luther encourages us to be patient with those
who don't yet grasp the way Christ exposes the inadequacy of
our righteousness and then covers us with *His* all-sufficient
righteousness. We may find ourselves like a rose among thorns,
a confident believer among unbelievers or believers struggling
for assurance. Luther warns us not to become proud because we
have trusted in Christ's righteousness. That would make us self-
righteous all over again, and turn us back into thorns. Luther
(1483–1546) was the German pastor, theologian, and former
monk whose rediscovery of the biblical view of justification
by faith sparked the Protestant Reformation.

I would like to know how it is with your soul, whether it has at
length learned to despise its own righteousness and seek comfort
and joy in Christ's righteousness. For, at present the temptation
to rest in one's own works is very powerful, especially among
those who long to be good and pious. They are ignorant of
God's righteousness, which has been so richly bestowed on us
in Christ without money and price, and try to do good of
themselves, until they imagine they can appear before God
adorned with every grace. But that is impossible. You, yourself,
when you were with us suffered from this illusion, or rather
delusion, and I also was a martyr to it. Even now I have not
entirely overcome it. Therefore, dear brother, learn Christ and

51

Him crucified. Praise his name and, despairing of yourself, say to him, 'You, Lord Jesus, are my righteousness, but I am your sin. You have taken what is mine, and given me what is yours. You have become that which you were not, and given me what I did not have.'

Beware, my brother, at aiming at a purity which rebels against being classed with sinners. For Christ only dwells among sinners. For this is the reason he came from heaven, where he dwelt among saints, so that he might also make his home with the sinful. Strive after such love, and you will experience his sweetest comfort. For if by our own efforts we are to attain peace of conscience, why then did Christ die? Therefore you will only find peace in him when you despair of yourself and your own works. He himself will teach you how in receiving you he makes your sins his, and his righteousness yours. When you believe this firmly (and those who do not believe it are damned) then bear patiently with wayward brothers and sisters. Make their sins your own responsibility. If there be any good in you, then 'welcome one another as Christ has welcomed you, for the glory of God' (Rom. 15:7). 'Have this mind among yourselves, which is yours in Christ Jesus, who, though he was in the form of God, did not count equality with God a thing to be grasped' (Phil. 2:5-6). You should have the same attitude. If you esteem yourself better than others, do not pride yourself on that, but be one with them, bearing their burdens. For he is a pitiable saint who will not bear patiently with those worse than himself, and longs only for solitude, when he, through patience, prayer, and example, might exercise a helpful influence over others. This is burying his Lord's talent, and not giving his fellow-servants their due.

Therefore, be a lily or rose of Christ, knowing that you must walk among thorns (Song 2:1-2). Only make sure you do not become a thorn again through impatience, hasty judgments, or secret pride! Christ rules, says the psalmist, in the midst of his enemies (Ps. 110:2). Why then rejoice when you are surrounded only by faithful friends? If he, your Lord, had only lived among the good, or had only died for his friends, for whom then would he have died, or with whom could he have lived!

- Can you see how illogical it is to feel superior towards people who don't grasp the grace of God?

16.

Charles Spurgeon on the Song of Songs 2:1-2

I am a rose of Sharon,
a lily of the valleys.
As a lily among brambles,
so is my love among the young women.

This extract is a prayer of confession taken from the conclusion of a sermon by Charles Spurgeon (see #7) on the Song of Songs 2:1-2. Unlike the interpretations promoted in the NIV and ESV, Spurgeon believed it is Jesus who speaks in verse 1, inviting us to consider his beauty. High thoughts of Christ, says Spurgeon, will increase our love, comfort our hearts, energise our souls, and inspire our service. Then, after sketching out why Christ is justified in commending Himself in this way, Spurgeon ends with this prayer of confession.

'My Lord, I am truly ashamed to think that I have not gazed more upon you. I know, and in my heart believe, that you are the total sum of all beauty. Yet I must sorrowfully lament that my eyes have been gadding about to look at other beauties; my thoughts have been deluded with imaginary excellencies in the creature; and I have meditated only a little upon yourself.

'Alas, my Lord, I confess still further that I have not possessed and enjoyed you as I ought! When I might have been with you all the day and all the night, I have been roving here and there, forgetting my resting place. I have not been careful to welcome my Beloved and to retain his company. I have stirred him up by my sins, and have driven him away by my lukewarmness.

I have given him cold lodgings and slender hospitality within the chambers of my heart. I have not held him fast, neither have I pressed him to abide with me as I should have done. All this, I must confess, and mourn that I am not more ashamed while confessing it.

'Moreover, my good Lord, although I know your great sacrifice for me, and might well have chained my heart forever to your altar (and oh that you had done so!), I must acknowledge that I have not been a living sacrifice as I should have been. I have not been so fascinated by the lustre of your beauty as I should have been. Oh that all my heart's rooms had been occupied by you, and by you alone! Would my soul were as the coals in the furnace, all on flame, and not a single particle of me left unconsumed by the delightful flames of your love.

'I must also confess, my Lord, that I have not spoken of you as I should have done. Although I have had many opportunities, yet I have not praised you at the rate which you deserve. I have given you at best but a poor, stammering, chilly tongue, when I should have spoken with the fiery zeal of a seraph.'

- Make this confession your own or continue it in your own words.

17.

Thomas Boston on the Song of Songs 2:3

As an apple tree among the trees of the forest,
so is my beloved among the young men.
With great delight I sat in his shadow.

Just as we stand in the shade of a tree to avoid the heat of the sun, says Thomas Boston, so we stand in the shade of Christ to avoid the heat of God's wrath. In Christ's shadow, God is no longer our threat, but our comfort. Boston (1676-1732) was a leading Scottish Presbyterian minister and theologian.

Adam's fall has changed the temperature of the air we breathe. God himself was the sun of the world, whose influences were enlightening, cheering, comforting and warming to innocent men, but has become a consuming fire to the workers of iniquity. He now darts his rays directly down upon the head of the sinner, so that the whole head is sick and the heart faint. It is become so hot that, if a shadow had not been provided, this world had all been burnt up before now.

But Christ became a shadow for poor sinners ... He received all the scorching beams of wrath on himself, so that he might keep them from his people. 'For our sake he made him to be sin who knew no sin, so that in him we might become the righteousness of God' (2 Cor. 5:21). Why is the person safe under the shadow, if not because the thick branches of the tree which make the shadow receive scorching beams of the hot sun which otherwise would reach them? The beams of wrath which should have scorched all the elect world were contracted in the covenant between the Father and the second Adam as in a magnifying glass, and so pointed directly on his head and concentrated in him. 'The LORD has laid on him the iniquity of us all' (Isa. 53:6) ... He exhausted them. He drank the cup of wrath from the brim to the bottom. So that there was no more revenging wrath to fall on him ...

And on this basis, our Lord Christ bids his people come away with him. For now the storm has blown over on him, the sky is clear, and there is safe travelling for guilty creatures to the throne of God (Song 2:10-11). Through him, the comforting influences of heaven are bestowed and conveyed to those under his shadow, through him as the channel of conveyance. The sun beats no more upon the tree with its great heat, but shines upon it fair and sweet, and will do so for ever. And so those under its shadow receive quieting, reviving, enlightening, and fruitful influences.

Come under Christ's shadow, you who fear the Lord's wrath. Here is a shadow for ease to you ... Come, tempted souls, whom Satan is plying with fiery darts. If you sit down under Christ's shadow by faith, it will be a defence to you ... Come, you whose corruptions are rampant. Christ's shadow will cool the distempered heat of your souls, and reduce them to a holy temperature ... Come all of you, whatever your case be.

- 'Come all of you, whatever your case be,' says Boston. What is your case today and how does the shadow of Christ protect or comfort you?

18.

Thomas Manton on the Song of Songs 2:3

With great delight I sat in his shadow,
and his fruit was sweet to my taste.

Sometimes people think of the gospel as simply cancelling out negatives: forgiving sin, appeasing wrath, escaping judgment. And, in exchange, we have to 'put up' with the burden of obedience. Not so, says Thomas Manton. We find pleasures in knowing Christ that outshine all other pleasures. Manton (1620-1677) was a Puritan minister and a clerk to the Westminster Assembly. He left the Church of England in 1662 at the Great Ejection, and was imprisoned for six months for unauthorised preaching.

There are many choice and excellent fruits which believers receive from Christ: the pardon of all our sins (Eph. 1:7); peace with God (Rom. 5:1); adoption into God's family (John 1:12, 1 John 3:1); the heirs of glory (Rom. 8:17); the Holy Spirit (1 Cor. 6:19); peace of conscience and joy in the Holy Spirit (Rom. 12:17); and access to God (Heb. 4:15-16).

They are his fruits because they are purchased by him. All these privileges were procured for us by his blood, death, and sufferings. He has the keeping and dispensing of these purchased benefits, for he has purchased this grace, not into another's hand, but into his own. By the Spirit he sanctifies and brings back the souls of people unto God (John 1:16). They are enjoyed by virtue of an interest in him, as we are members of his mystical body (1 Cor. 1:30) ...

We entertain dark thoughts of the ways of God, as if religion were a sour thing, and there were no pleasure and delight for those that submit to it ... Oh, taste and see! You will find enough in Christ to spoil the relish of all other pleasures. As the sun puts out the fire, so does this greater delight make carnal vanities tasteless. Surely all Christ's fruits will be sweet to you ... We are never so pleased as when we enjoy most of God, and have a sense of his presence. We are never so satisfied as when we are most fruitful, when most powerfully drawn towards God. This taste must be cherished, and kept up in us. Affectionate stirrings and workings of soul after heavenly things are very sweet, and all Christians should strive for them.

Yet esteem, choice, thorough willingness and being satisfied in Christ are the main things. You must not be dead-hearted. Therefore you must take heed of those things which would deaden your taste ... Till sin grow bitter to us, nothing in Christ will have relish for us. For Christ came to take sin away and, till sin be sin indeed, grace will never be grace indeed ... Prepare your appetite by self-examining (1 Cor. 11:28), and confession of sin. Humiliation for our unworthiness, reconciling ourselves to God upon new covenant terms, heartfelt resolutions for God, a deep sense of our wants – these things breed an appetite and desire for grace. And hungry consciences know how to prize the food.

- Ask God to make sin grow more bitter to your taste, and to make Christ more sweet. You might want to mention a specific sin with which you struggle.

19.

Alexander Moody Stuart on the Song of Songs 2:4

He brought me to the banqueting house,
and his banner over me was love.

Alexander Moody Stuart (see #10) says the banner in this verse
marks the conquest of Christ over His people. But this is a
victory that has been won through love. This is like a man
winning the heart of his bride, rather than an army enforcing
its will on an enemy. There is one sense in which military
imagery is appropriate: the banner is also the banner under
which we now fight as soldiers of Christ. Yet, even here, we
fight not with conventional weapons, but with 'the warfare
of love'.

'And his banner over me was love' – and *is* love, for it continues
floating over her still.

It is the banner of *conquest* over you, believer, by which he
subdued you to himself; by which he conquered you when you
were in hatred, in rebellion, in arms against him. It was he that
disarmed you, he that subdued and took you captive. Commands
you met with resistance, righteous anger with unholy enmity,
threatened vengeance with servile fear and flight. Law arrested
you, fettered you, silenced you, slew you; without it you had
previously made light of all the tenderness of love. But the
law never completely disarmed your resistance. It was love that
called to you in your rebellious flight, and turned you to reason
together with your Lord. Love allured you to look upon the
righteousness of law, and to accept the justice of judgment.

Love kindly drew aside the veil of prejudice from your eyes, gently yet irresistibly took the arms of war out of your hands, the arguments of self-vindication from your lips, the gall of bitterness out of your heart. He loved you, you believed in his love, and being overcome you loved him again who first loved you. Having conquered you by love, he erected over you love's triumphal banner.

It is the banner also of *protection*. He has planted it firmly over you; your enemies see it and are afraid, the god of the world and the children of the world fear to touch you beneath this ensign ... So, believer, still Satan and the world fear that love, and fear you when that banner floats over you. Thus, also, within your own soul 'the peace of God, which surpasses all understanding, will guard your hearts and your minds in Christ Jesus' (Phil. 4:7), keeps you, protects you, preserves you more than with a wall of fire. O tear not this banner down, disown it not, but let your soul make her boast in the Lord, believing in his love.

It is the banner also of *enlistment*, for Christ has chosen you to be his soldier, and the banner under which he has enrolled you to serve is Love. In the legion of love he has inscribed your name, and the warfare of love he has called you to wage. His best soldiers are those who love best; who, through love, 'endure everything for the sake of the elect' (2 Tim. 2:10), through love 'become all things to all people, that by all means they might save some' (1 Cor. 9:22), who in love 'is patient and kind ... bears all things, believes all things, hopes all things, endures all things' (1 Cor. 13:4, 7), and by love 'overcomes evil with good' (Rom. 12:21) When all other weapons in your armoury have failed, love will triumph.

- What might it mean for you today to engage in 'the warfare of love'?

20.

Matthew Henry on the Song of Songs 2:5-7

Sustain me with raisins;
refresh me with apples,
for I am sick with love.
His left hand is under my head,
and his right hand embraces me!
I adjure you, O daughters of Jerusalem,
by the gazelles or the does of the field,
that you not stir up or awaken love
until it pleases.

Once we have tasted the joy of Christ's love, we find we can't live without it! Even when our sense of His love is weak, says Matthew Henry, Christ still sustains us. And when we *do* sense His love, we should avoid doing anything that might bring that experience to a premature end. Henry (1662-1714) was a Welsh nonconformist minister who is best known for his commentary on the Bible.

The bride professes her strong affection and most passionate love to Jesus Christ: 'I am sick with love,' overcome, overpowered, by it. David explains this when he says, 'My soul is consumed with longing for your rules at all times' (Ps. 119:20) and 'My soul faints with longing for your salvation' (Ps. 119:81 NIV), languishing with care to make it sure and fear of coming short of it. The spouse was now absent perhaps from her beloved, waiting for his return, and cannot bear the grief of distance and delay. Oh how much better it is with the soul when it is 'sick with love' for Christ than when it is surfeited with the love of this world! She cries out for cordials: 'Oh *sustain me with raisins* (or *flagons*, or *ointments*, or *flowers*), anything that is reviving; *refresh me with apples*, with the fruits of that *apple tree* which is Christ (verse 3), with the merit and meditation of Christ and the sense of his love to my soul.' Notice that those that are 'sick with love' for Christ shall not lack spiritual supports, even while they are waiting for spiritual comforts.

She experiences the power and tenderness of divine grace, relieving her in her present faintings (verse 6). Though he seemed to have withdrawn, yet he was still a very present help. He was present to sustain the love-sick soul, and to keep it from fainting away: '*His left hand is under my head*, to bear it up, nay, as a pillow to lay it easy.' David experienced God's hand upholding him then when his soul was following hard after God (Ps. 63:8 KJV), and Job in a state of desertion nevertheless found that God 'put strength' into him (Job 23:6 KJV). All his saints are in his hand, which tenderly holds their aching heads. To encourage the love-sick soul to continue waiting till he returns, 'his right hand embraces me' in the meantime, and thereby gives an unquestionable assurance of his love. Believers owe all their strength and comfort to the supporting left hand and embracing right hand of the Lord Jesus.

Finding her beloved near to her in verse 7 she takes great care that her communion with him is not interrupted. 'I adjure you, O you daughters of Jerusalem.' Jerusalem, the mother of us all, charges all her daughters, the church charges all her members, the believing soul charges all its powers and faculties, the spouse charges herself and all about her, not to 'stir not up, nor awake my love, till he please' (KJV), now that he is asleep in her arms, as she was borne up in his (verse 6). She gives them this charge 'by the gazelles or the does of the field', that is, by every thing that is amiable in their eyes, and dear to them, as the loving hind and the pleasant roe. 'My love is to me dearer than those can be to you, and will be disturbed, like them, with a very little noise.'

Notice that those who experience the sweetness of communion with Christ, and the sensed manifestations of his love, cannot but desire the continuation of these blessed views and these blessed visits (just as Peter wanted to make tabernacles on the mount of transfiguration in Matthew 17:4). Yet Christ will, when he pleases, withdraw these extraordinary communications of himself, for he is a free-agent, and the Spirit like the wind 'blows where' – and when – 'it wishes' (John 3:8). It is appropriate then for us to acquiesce to his pleasure. But, our care must be to ensure we do nothing to provoke him to withdraw and to hide his face, that we carefully watch over our own hearts and suppress every thought that may grieve his good Spirit. Let those that have comfort be afraid of sinning it away.

- Are you enjoying a sense of Christ's love? What might you do that would bring it to a premature end?

21.

Thomas Brooks on the Song of Songs 2:8

The voice of my beloved!
Behold, he comes,
leaping over the mountains,
bounding over the hills.

Before we could enjoy communion with Him, Christ had to overcome sin, judgment, and death. They were like mountains standing in the way, says Thomas Brooks, but Christ leapt over them. So we should not let any obstacles stand in our way of coming to Him. Brooks (1608-1680) was a Puritan preacher who is best known for his works *Precious Remedies Against Satan's Devices* and *Heaven on Earth*.

Let all gracious and upright hearts consider this, that Jesus Christ has persisted in a way of mercy and sweetness towards you, notwithstanding all the discouragements and all the obstacles that have been in his way. And will you not persist in ways of duty to Christ, who has persisted, notwithstanding all discouragements, in a way of mercy towards you?

Consider what difficulties the Lord Jesus Christ has gone through to come to your souls. In Song 2:8 it says, 'Behold, he comes, leaping over the mountains, bounding over the hills.' Oh the Lord Jesus Christ has come over mountains of wrath, mountains of sin, and mountains of sorrow, and all that he might come to your souls ... Oh the Lord, in a way of mercy towards you, has come over all difficulties. Jesus Christ never pleaded: 'Oh this mountain of wrath, of sin, and sorrow is too high for me to go over, and these valleys of darkness are too long and too terrible for me to walk through.' No, the Lord came skipping over all mountains, and all for the good of your souls.

And will not you, upright hearts, persist in ways of duty to him that has thus carried himself in ways of mercy to you? And as he has, so does he still persist in ways of mercy and kindness to you, notwithstanding all your provocations. Witness all those mercies that now you enjoy – the clothes you wear, and the bread you eat, and the house you lodge in, and the bed you lie on – when thousands lie down in everlasting sorrow ... Oh, this should exhort you to persist in his ways, notwithstanding any difficulties that you may meet along the way ...

Oh remember, upright souls, in the day of your marriage with Jesus Christ, you covenanted with the Lord Jesus Christ to keep close to him, to hold on in his ways ... In effect you said, 'Blessed Lord! I will follow you wherever you go; where you go I will go; and where you lodge I will lodge; and your God shall be my God; and nothing shall part between you and my soul, between your ways and my heart.' Therefore let that exhort you to persist in ways of well-doing, notwithstanding all afflictions and discouragements you meet in doing so.

- What prevents you from coming to Christ in prayer? What motives are there for you to overcome those obstacles?

22.

Robert Murray M'Cheyne on the Song of Songs 2:8-9

The voice of my beloved!
Behold, he comes,
leaping over the mountains,
bounding over the hills.
My beloved is like a gazelle
or a young stag.

Whereas Thomas Brooks focused on Christ opening up a way for us to meet Him through His death and resurrection (see #21), Robert Murray M'Cheyne focuses on the subjective experience this creates; the experience of Christ coming to us with a fresh sense of His love and comfort. M'Cheyne (1813-1843) was the minister at St Peter's Church in Dundee. Despite dying of ill-health at just twenty-nine, he has exercised considerable influence through his passion and piety. This extract is from the first sermon he preached at St Peter's, when he was still a candidate.

Christ's coming to the desolate believer is often sudden and wonderful ... It was when the bride was sitting lonely and desolate that she suddenly heard the voice of her Lord. Love is quick in hearing; and she cries out, 'The voice of my beloved!' Before she thought the mountains all but impassable. But now she can compare his swiftness to nothing but that of the gazelle or the young stag. Yes, while she speaks, he is at the wall - at the window - showing himself through the lattice. It is often like this with believers. While they sit alone and desolate, the mountains of separation appear a vast and impassable barrier to the Saviour, and they fear he may never come again.

The mountains of a believer's provocations are often very great. 'That I should have sinned again, who have been washed in the blood of Jesus. It is a small thing that other people should sin against him; they never knew him – never loved him as I have done. Surely I am the chief of sinners, and have sinned away my Saviour. The mountain of my provocations has grown up to heaven, and he will never come over it any more.' Thus it is that believers write bitter things against themselves.

And then it is that often they hear the voice of their beloved. Some text of God's word, or some word from a Christian friend, or some part of a sermon, again reveals Jesus in all his fulness – the Saviour of sinners, even the chief. Or it may be that he makes himself known to the disconsolate soul in the breaking of bread, and when he speaks the gentle words, 'This is my body. This is my blood of the new covenant, which is poured out for many for the forgiveness of sins. Drink of it, all of you.' Then believers cannot but cry out, 'The voice of my beloved! Behold, he comes, leaping over the mountains, bounding over the hills.'

Ah, my friends, do you know anything of this joyful surprise? If you do, why should you ever sit in despair ... Come with expectancy to the word. Do not come with a listless indifference, as if nothing that a fellow-worm can say were worth your hearing. It is not the word of man, but the word of the living God. Come with large expectations, and then you will find the promise true, that he fills the hungry with good things, though he sends the rich empty away (Luke 1:53).

- M'Cheyne speaks of 'some text of God's word, or some word from a Christian friend, or some part of a sermon', or 'the breaking of bread' revealing Jesus afresh to us in all His fulness. When was the last time you experienced something like this?

23.

Martin Luther on the Song of Songs 2:9

My beloved is like a gazelle
or a young stag.
Behold, there he stands
behind our wall,
gazing through the windows,
looking through the lattice.

Martin Luther (see #15) takes the picture of the beloved standing behind a wall as a picture of the way Christ is hidden behind sufferings. Adversity might suggest Christ is absent or angry, but faith remains confident that Christ is present in love. That's because Christ allows Himself to be seen 'through the window', and because faith recognises the way God uses suffering for our good.

Let us consider people who suffer in body, property, honour, friends, or whatever they have. Do they still believe they are pleasing to God? Do they believe God in his mercy appoints their sufferings and difficulties, whether small or great? This is real strength: to trust in God when to all our senses and reason he appears to be angry; and to have greater confidence in him than we feel. Here he is hidden, as the bride says in the Song of Songs: 'Behold, there he stands behind our wall, gazing through the windows' (2:9)

He stands hidden among our sufferings, which appear to separate us from him like a wall, like a wall of stone. And yet he looks upon me and does not leave me, for he is standing and is ready to help in his grace. And through the window of dim faith he allows himself to be seen. Jeremiah says in Lamentations 3:31-33 (NIV):

> For no one is cast off
> by the LORD forever.
> Though he brings grief, he will show compassion,
> so great is his unfailing love.
> For he does not willingly bring affliction
> or grief to anyone.

Some people do not have this faith, and give up. They assume God has forsaken them and has become their enemy. They blame their problems on people and devils, and have no confidence at all in God. For this reason, too, their suffering is always an offence and harmful to them. And then they go out and do what they think are good works with no awareness of their unbelief.

But others trust God in suffering and retain a good, firm confidence in him, believing he is pleased with them. These people see in their sufferings and afflictions nothing but precious merits and the rare treasures, the value of which no one can estimate. For faith and confidence make precious before God what others think to be shameful. So it is written even of death in Psalm 116:15: 'Precious in the sight of the LORD is the death of his faithful servants (NIV).'

And, just as the confidence and faith are better, higher and stronger at this stage than in the first stage, so in the same way sufferings which are borne in faith exceed all others works of faith. Therefore the fruit produced through suffering is much superior to anything produced by works.

- Are you facing struggles today? Ask Christ to strengthen your faith so you can be confident He is working for your good through your difficulties.

24.

Gregory of Nyssa on the Song of Songs 2:10-13

My beloved speaks and says to me:
'Arise, my love, my beautiful one,
and come away,
for behold, the winter is past;
the rain is over and gone.
The flowers appear on the earth,
the time of singing has come,
and the voice of the turtledove
is heard in our land.
The fig tree ripens its figs,
and the vines are in blossom;
they give forth fragrance.'

Gregory of Nyssa (see #8) says we live between the barren winter of the reign of sin and the glorious summer harvest when Christ returns. In between, spring has come with the resurrection of Christ. While perfection ('the full fruits of virtue') is not yet possible because the summer of Christ's return has not yet come, we can adorn ourselves with the 'flowers' of faith because, for us, the winter of sin's reign is past.

The Word has spoken to her and called her 'fair one' because she is close to him and 'dove' because of her beauty. And he continues by saying in the words that follow that the misery of the soul's winter does not triumph, because the frost fails to withstand the radiance. 'For behold,' he says, 'the winter is past, the rain is over and gone' ...

But understand these afflictions of the winter season, and everything that is like them, by taking them in a transferred, figural sense ... The human race flourished at the beginning, while it was lodged in the paradise, nurtured by the water of that spring and flourishing. At that time, its nature was adorned not with leaves but with the blossom of immortality. But the winter of disobedience dried up the root. The blossom was shaken off and fell to the earth; the human being was stripped of the beauty of immortality, and the green grass of the virtues was dried up as love for God became cold in the face of burgeoning lawlessness ...

But then there came the One who works in us the springtime of souls ... Once again our nature began to flourish and to be adorned with its own blossoms ... 'You see,' he says, 'the meadow blooming because of the virtues; you see self-control, that is, the bright and fragrant lily; you see reverence, the red rose; you see the violet, the sweet smell of Christ. Why, then, do you not employ these to make wreaths? This is the time at which it is right, the time when the cutting is done, to take pleasure in the plaiting of such wreaths' ...

The Word is describing the spiritual springtime to the Bride, and since this season is a halfway house between two others – between wintry desolation and the summer's sharing in the harvest – for just that reason, while he openly proclaims the passing of evil things, he does not yet point to the full fruits of virtue. These, however, he will dispense at the proper season, when the summer is come (and what 'summer' means, you know well enough from the words of the Lord, which say, 'The harvest is the consummation of the age' [Matt. 13:39]). But now what he manifests is the hopes that come to blossom through the virtues, whose fruit (as the prophet says) is brought forth in due season (Ps. 1:3).

Since, then, our human nature, like the fig tree that is mentioned here, has gathered to itself during the winter ... a great deal of harmful moisture, it is right that he who works in us the springtime of the soul and who cultivates the soil of our humanity by his husbandry should first of all cast out of our nature everything that is earthy and inappropriate, getting rid not of boughs but of transgressions through the act of confession, and then should proclaim the coming sweetness of the figs as he stamps in our being an impress of the hoped-for happiness by means of a more honourable life – an impress not unlike the early figs. This is what it means to say: *the fig tree has put forth its early fruit.*

- What are the dangers of thinking it is still winter (i.e. that sin still reigns over our lives), or thinking summer has come (i.e. that sin has no influence on us)?

25.

Robert Murray M'Cheyne on the Song of Songs 2:14

'O my dove, in the clefts of the rock,
in the crannies of the cliff,
let me see your face,
let me hear your voice,
for your voice is sweet,
and your face is lovely.'

Robert Murray M'Cheyne (see #22) invites us to hide in the wounds of Christ like a dove hiding in the cleft of the rock. By this, M'Cheyne means entrusting ourselves to the work of Christ on the cross, so that we are cleansed by His blood and healed by His wounds.

A timorous dove pursued by the vulture, and well-nigh made a prey, with fluttering anxious wing, hides itself deeper than ever in the clefts of the rock, and in the secret places of the precipice. In the same way, the backslidden believer, whom Satan has desired to have that he might sift him as wheat, when he is restored once more to the all-gracious presence of his Lord, clings to him with fluttering, anxious faith, and hides himself deeper than ever in the wounds of his Saviour.

Thus it was that the fallen Peter, when he had so grievously denied his Lord, was the only one of the disciples who cast himself into the sea to swim to Jesus. And that backslidden apostle, when again he had hidden himself in the clefts of the Rock of Ages, found that the love of Jesus was more tender towards him than ever.

Just so does every backslidden believer find that, when again he is hidden in the freshly opened wounds of his Lord, the fountain of his love begins to flow afresh, and the stream of kindness and affection is fuller and more overflowing than ever. For his word is, 'O my dove, in the clefts of the rock, in the crannies of the cliff, let me see your face, let me hear your voice, for your voice is sweet, and your face is lovely.'

My friends, do you know anything of this? Have you ever experienced such a coming of Jesus over the mountain of your provocations, as made a change of season to your soul? And have you, backslidden believer, found, when you hid yourself again deeper than ever in the clefts of the rock – like Peter girding his fisher's coat unto him, and casting himself into the sea – have you found his love more tender than ever to your soul?

Then should this not teach you to be quick to repent when you have fallen? Why keep one moment away from the Saviour? Are you waiting till you wipe away the stain from your garments? Alas, what will wipe it off, but the blood you are despising? Are you waiting till you make yourself more worthy of the Saviour's favour? Alas, though you wait until all eternity, you can never make yourself more worthy. Your sin and misery are your only plea. Come, and you will find with what tenderness he will heal your backslidings, and love you freely, and say, 'O my dove ... let me see your face, let me hear your voice.'

- 'He was pierced for our transgressions ... and by his wounds we are healed.' (Isa. 53:5 NIV)

26.

Matthew Henry on the Song of Songs 2:15

'Catch the foxes for us,
the little foxes
that spoil the vineyards,
for our vineyards are in blossom.'

'The little foxes' represent anything that might spoil our relationship with Christ. Matthew Henry (see #20) highlights two such threats. The first is internal: our own sinful desires and passions. He encourages us to turn from sin as soon as we see it rising in our hearts. The second threat is external: false teaching. While it is not our job to destroy false teachers (Christ will do so when He returns), we are to counter their influence.

This charge to 'catch the foxes' is, firstly, a charge to particular believers to put to death their own corruptions, their sinful appetites and passions. For these are like 'little foxes' that destroy their graces and comforts, quash good intentions, crush good beginnings, and prevent their coming to perfection. Seize the 'little foxes', the first risings of sin, the little ones of Babylon (Ps. 137:9), those sins that seem little, for they often prove very dangerous. Whatever we find a hindrance to us in that which is good we must put away.

Secondly, it is a charge to all Christians wherever they are to oppose and prevent the spreading of any opinions and practices that have a tendency to corrupt people's judgments, debauch their consciences, perplex their minds, and discourage their inclinations to virtue and piety. Persecutors are foxes (Luke 13:32), and false prophets are foxes (Ezek. 13:4). Those that sow the tares of heresy or schism, and, like Diotrephes (3 John 9-10), trouble the peace of the church and obstruct the progress of the gospel, are the *foxes, the little foxes*. They must not be knocked on the head for Christ did not come 'to destroy men's lives' (Luke 9:56 KJV). Instead, they may be tamed, or else restrained from doing mischief.

- Can you detect 'the first risings of sin' in your heart today? Turn from that sin in repentance by turning to Christ in faith.

27.

Martin Luther on the Song of Songs 2:16

My beloved is mine, and I am his;
he grazes among the lilies.

The Song of Songs describes the betrothal of believers to Christ in marriage, and in marriage a couple share all things in common. So Martin Luther (see #15) invites us to consider the benefits we receive from Christ, and our liabilities, for which He takes responsibility.

Faith unites the soul to Christ, like a wife to her husband. By this mystery, as the Apostle Paul teaches, Christ and the soul are made one flesh. Indeed their union is not only a true marriage, it is the most perfect of all marriages – since human marriages are merely faint pictures of this one great marriage. If, then, they are married in this way, it follows that all they have they now share in common, good things as well evil things. So whatever Christ possesses, the believing soul may claim and boast of as its own. And whatever belongs to the soul, Christ claims as his.

If we compare what each person possesses, then we shall see how incalculable the benefits are that we receive from Christ. Christ is full of grace, life and salvation; the soul is full of sin, death and condemnation. Let faith step in, and as a result our sin, death and hell now belong to Christ, and his grace, life and salvation belong to the soul. For if he is a husband, then he must needs take to himself what belongs to his wife and at the same time give to his wife what belongs to him. For, in giving her his very self, how can he not also give her all that is his?

And in taking to himself the body of his wife, how can he but take to himself all that is hers?

In this is displayed the delightful sight, not only of communion with Christ, but a triumphant battle which leads to victory, salvation and redemption. For Christ is God and man. He is a person who has neither sinned, nor dies, nor is condemned. Indeed, he cannot sin, die, or be condemned. His righteousness, life and salvation are invincible, eternal and almighty. And now this person, through the wedding-ring of faith, treats the sins, death and hell of his wife as his own. He deals with them as if they were his, and as if he himself had sinned. He suffers, dies and descends to hell, so that he may overcome all things. And since sin, death and hell cannot swallow him up, they must instead be swallowed up by him in stupendous conflict. For his righteousness rises above human sins; his life is more powerful than all of death; his salvation is more invincible than all of hell.

Thus the believing soul, by the pledge of its faith in Christ, becomes free from all sin, fearless of death, safe from hell, and receives the eternal righteousness, life and salvation of its husband Christ. Thus Christ presents to himself a glorious bride, without spot or wrinkle, cleansing her with the washing of water by the word; that is, by faith in the word of life, righteousness, and salvation (Eph. 5:26-27). Thus he becomes engaged to her 'in righteousness and in justice, in steadfast love and in mercy' (Hos. 2:19-20).

Who then can put a price on this royal wedding? Who can comprehend the riches of the glory of this grace? Christ, that rich and pious husband, takes as his wife a needy and impious prostitute, redeeming her from all her evils and supplying her with all his good things. It is impossible now for her sins to ruin her since they have been laid on Christ and swallowed up in him. She has in her husband Christ a righteousness which she may claim as her own. So she stands up with confidence against all her sins, against death and hell, saying, 'If I have sinned, my

Christ, in whom I believe, has not sinned; all mine is his, and all his is mine.' As it is written: 'My beloved is mine, and I am his.'

- Consider the challenges or problems or fears that you face. Then respond by saying, 'My beloved is mine, and I am his.'

28.

Alexander Moody Stuart on the Song of Songs 2:16

My beloved is mine, and I am his;
he grazes among the lilies.

Like Martin Luther (see #27), Alexander Moody Stuart (see #10) encourages us to consider what is ours if Christ is ours. He also encourages us to consider to whom we do *not* belong, now that we belong to Christ.

It is true of every follower and lover of the Lord Jesus Christ, whether you know it or not, that your Beloved is yours. For ever and ever you shall sing, 'My Beloved is mine,' and you may sing it as assuredly now. He is mine by the free gift of himself to me. He is mine to look on, to lean upon, to dwell with. He is mine to bear all my burdens, mine to discharge all my debts, mine to answer all my accusers, mine to conquer all my foes. He is mine to deliver me from hell, mine to prepare a place for me in heaven. He is mine in absence, mine in presence. He is mine in life, mine in death, mine in the grave, mine in the judgment, and mine at the marriage of the Lamb.

And I am his. I am his, by him created; and I am his, by him redeemed. I am twice his: by original right and by purchase when I was lost. I am his by the ransom of his blood, his by the conquest of his Spirit, his by my own free consent. I am his in body, in soul, in estate. I am his entirely, his exclusively, his irrevocably. I am his and he will defend me, his and he will correct me, his and he will make use of me. I am his and he will love me, his and he will delight in me, his and he will claim me against all rivals and opponents. Indeed, I am his and he now loves me, his and he now delights in me, his and he now claims me against all adversaries. I am not my own, not the church's, not the world's, not another person's, not the law's, not Satan's, but his, Christ's, my Beloved's. I am not the property of time, nor of care, nor of business, nor of necessity, but of Christ, for I am his. All things, O believer, are yours in Christ, yet you are no one's but his. All things belong to you, but you belong to none but Jesus. You are the property of no person, the property of no creature, the property of no uncreated, yet mighty reality, like sin. I am my Beloved's, and no one else possesses either right or power over me, except according to his will and sanction. And, if I am my Beloved's and he is mine, then all that is mine is his – all my sin, my weakness, my condemnation, and my misery. And all that is his is mine – all his strength, his righteousness, his wisdom, his holiness, his salvation, his glory. His God is my God, his Father is my Father, his family is my family, his heaven is my home.

- Do you feel under pressure today – from yourself, other people, the wider culture, or the law or Satan? In response, declare aloud: 'I am not yours; I belong to Christ!'

29.

Bernard of Clairvaux on the Song of Songs 2:17

Until the day breathes
and the shadows flee,
turn, my beloved, be like a gazelle
or a young stag on cleft mountains.

To help his monks, Bernard of Clairvaux (see #5) describes what it has meant for him to have an experience of Christ's presence. But it is hard to find the right words; neither the language of 'coming from outside', nor 'being present within', do justice to an encounter with God. But we can know we have experienced God when we have felt the warmth of His love or the exposure of our sin. And when we sense no longer His presence, we long for His return – just like the bride in the Song.

Bear with my foolishness for a little (2 Cor. 11:17). I want to tell you, as I promised, how I have experienced the presence of the Word in me ... Although he has frequently entered my soul, I have never at any time been aware of the precise moment of his coming. I have felt that he was present. I remember that he has been with me. I have sometimes even had an inkling that he would come. But I have never actually felt his coming, nor his departure (Ps. 121:8). From where he came to enter my soul, or where he went when he left it, or by what means he entered or departed, I confess I do not know even to this day. As it says, 'you do not know where it comes from or where it goes' (John 3:8). Nor is this surprising, because it is to him that the

87

Psalmist said: 'your footprints were unseen' (Ps. 77:19). He did not enter through my eyes, for he is without form or colour that eyes can discern; nor through my ears, for his coming is without sound; nor through my nostrils, for he is not mingled with the air but with the mind. He has not simply acted upon the air, for he created it. Nor did he enter through my mouth, since he is not made of something that can be eaten or drunk. Finally, he could not be detected through touch since he is intangible. So by what route has he entered?

Or perhaps he did not *enter* at all because he did not come from outside. Yet he has not come from within me, for he is good, and 'I know that nothing good dwells in me' (Rom. 7:18). I have ascended higher than myself, and yet I have found the Word above me still. My curiosity has led me to descend below myself, and yet again I have found him deeper still. If I have looked outside of myself, I have found him to be beyond that which is outside of me; and if I look within, he was further in still. And so I have learned the truth of the words I had read: 'In him we live and move and have our being' (Act 17:28). But blessed is the one who lives for him, and is moved by him, and has their being in him.

You will ask, then, since his access into my soul can be traced, how I know he was present? He is living and full of energy, and as soon as he has entered he has given life to my sleeping soul. He has aroused and softened and provoked my heart, which was in a state of lethargy, and hard as a stone. He has begun to root out and destroy, to plant and to build, to water the dry places, to illuminate the gloomy spots, to throw open that which was shut, to inflame with warmth that which was cold, to straighten crooked paths and make rough places smooth, so that my soul might bless the Lord, and all that is within me praise his holy name (Ps. 103:1).

Thus, the Bridegroom-Word, though he has entered me several times, has never made his coming apparent to my sight, hearing, or touch. It was not by his movements that I recognised him, nor could I tell by any of my senses that he had penetrated to the depths of my being. It was, as I have already said, only by the renewed warmth of my heart that I was able to recognise his presence. I knew the power of his sacred presence because the power of my vices departed and my fleshly carnal affections were restrained. From the discovery and conviction of my secret faults I have had good reason to admire the depth of his wisdom. His goodness and kindness have been made known through the amendment of my life, limited though that is. While through the reforming and renewing of my mind (that is, my inward man), I have perceived to a certain extent the excellency of the Divine beauty. And as I meditated on all these things, I have been filled with wonder and amazement at his greatness and majesty.

But when the Word withdrew, all these spiritual powers and faculties began to droop and languish, as if the fire had been withdrawn from a boiling cooking pot. And this is to me the sign of his departure. Then inevitably my soul is sad and despondent until he returns and my heart grows warm within me again, as it does, to show that he has returned. After having experienced such happiness from the indwelling Word, it is hardly surprising that I should adopt the language of the Bride in the Song of Song when she recalls her Beloved after he has departed. That's because I am driven by desire, perhaps not as powerful as hers, but at least similar to it? As long as I live her words shall be in my mind, and shall be what I use to call upon the Word, that word which I find here: 'Return.'

- 'Father, strengthen me with power through your Spirit in my inner being, so that Christ may dwell in my heart through faith.' (From Eph. 3:16-17)

30.

Charles Spurgeon on the Song of Songs 2:17

Until the day breathes
and the shadows flee,
turn, my beloved, be like a gazelle
or a young stag on cleft mountains.

We do not always have experiences of Christ's presence. Indeed, says Charles Spurgeon (see #7), sometimes Christians have an experience of Christ's *absence*. We can feel very alone, or even abandoned by Christ. Spurgeon himself struggled with bouts of depression. Whether we ourselves feel like we are in darkness or we feel the darkness over the church, Spurgeon encourages us to receive this verse as a promise that the darkness will not last forever.

The spouse sings, 'Until the day breathes and the shadows flee.' So the beloved of the Lord may be in the dark. It may be night with her who has a place in the heart of the Well-beloved. A child of God, who is a child of light, may be for a while in darkness ...

Yes, it may be very black with them, and they may be obliged to cry, 'I see no signs of returning day.' Sometimes, neither sun nor moon appears for a long season to cheer the believer in the dark. This may arise partly through sickness of body. There are sicknesses of the body which, in a very peculiar way, touch the soul. Yet exquisite pain may be attended with great brightness and joy. But there are certain other illnesses which influence us in another way. Terrible depression comes over us; we walk in darkness, and see no light ... It is not always that a person can gather themselves together, and defy these fierce blasts, and walk through fire and water with heavenly equanimity. No, brothers and sisters, 'a crushed spirit who can bear?' (Prov. 18:14) And that wounded spirit may be the portion of some of the very fairest of the children of God. Indeed, the Lord has some weakly, sickly children who, nevertheless, are the very pick of his family. It is not always the strong ones by whom he sets the most store, but, sometimes, those that seem to be driven into a corner, whose days are spent in mourning, are among the most precious in his sight.

But yet it can only be temporary darkness. The same text that suggests night promises dawn: 'Until the day breathes and the shadows flee,' says the song of the spouse. Perhaps no text is more frequently on my lips than is this one. I do not think that any passage of Scripture more often recurs in my heart when I am alone, for just now I feel that there is a gathering gloom over the church and over the world. It seems as if night were coming on, and such a night as makes one sigh and cry, 'Until the day breathes and the shadows flee' ...

Let me encourage any friends who have been labouring for Christ in any district which has seemed strikingly barren, where the stones of the field have seemed to break the ploughshare. Still believe on, beloved. That soil which appears most unfruitful will perhaps repay us after a while with a hundred-fold harvest. The prospect may be dark; perhaps, dear friends, it is to be darker yet with us. We may have worked, and seemed to work in vain. Possibly the vanity of all our working is yet to appear still more. But, for all that, the morning is coming. 'Those who sow in tears shall reap with shouts of joy!' (Ps. 126:5) We must not be in the least bit afraid, even in the densest darkness, but on the contrary look for the coming blessing ...

'Turn to me, O my Beloved, for you have turned away from me, or from your church. Turn again, I beg you. Pardon my lukewarmness, forgive my indifference. Turn to me again, my

Beloved. O you Husband of my soul, if I have grieved you, and you have hidden your face from me, turn again to me! Smile again at me, for then shall the day break, and the shadows flee away. Come to me, my Lord, visit me once again.'

- Make Spurgeon's closing prayer your own today.

31.

Walter Hilton on the Song of Songs 3:1

On my bed by night
I sought him whom my soul loves;
I sought him, but found him not.

Walter Hilton says Christ sometimes hides His presence from
us to strengthen our desire for Him – a theme also common in
the writings of the Puritans. But when Christ has accomplished
His purposes in a soul, He returns. Hilton then picks up the
imagery of the Song 1:2: 'Your name is oil poured out.' The
word *Jesus* means 'salvation' or 'health'. So Hilton says Christ's
return is like healing oil, bringing health to the soul. Hilton
(d. 1396) was an Augustinian monk.

His hiding is but a subtle trying of the soul. His showing is a
wonderful merciful goodness in comforting the soul. Wonder
not though the feelings of grace be sometimes withdrawn from
a lover of Jesus. For holy Scripture says the same of the Spouse,
that it fares thus with her: 'I sought him, but found him not'
(3:1). That is, when I fall down to my frailty and sin, then grace
withdraws. My falling is the cause of it, and not his flying. But
then I feel the pain of my wretchedness in his absence. And,
therefore, I sought him by great desire of heart, and he gave to
me not so much as a feeble answer. Then I cried with all my
soul, 'Turn, my beloved' (2:17). And yet it seemed as if he heard
me not. The painful feeling of myself, and the assault of fleshly
loves and fears in this time, and the wanting of my spiritual
strength, is a continual crying of my soul to Jesus. Nevertheless

our Lord makes strange, and does not come, no matter how much I cry. For he is not yet sure that I will not turn again to worldly loves and can have no savour in them, and, therefore, he stays away the longer.

But at the last, when he pleases, he comes again full of grace and truth (John 1:14). He visits the soul that languishes through desire, through sighs of love after his presence. And he touches it, and anoints it gently with the oil of gladness, and makes it suddenly whole from all pain. And then cries the soul to Jesus in a spiritual voice with a glad heart thus: 'Your name is oil poured out' (Song 1:2).

'Your name is *Jesus*, that is, "health". Then as long as I feel my soul sore and sick by reason of sin, pained with the heavy burden of my body, sorrowful and fearful for the perils and wretchedness of this life, so long, Lord Jesus, your name is oil shut up, not poured forth. But when I feel my soul suddenly touched with the light of your grace, healed and cured from all the filth of sin, and comforted in love and in light with spiritual strength and gladness unspeakable, then can I say with lusty, loving and spiritual might to you: "Your name, O Jesus, is to me oil poured out. For, by the effect of your gracious visit, I truly feel the exposition of your name, that you are *Jesus*, 'health', for only your gracious presence heals me from sorrow and from sin."'

Happy is that soul that is ever fed with the feeling of love in his presence, or is borne up by desire to him in his absence. A wise lover is he, and well taught, that soberly and reverently behaves himself in his presence, and lovingly beholds him without dissolute lightness, and patiently and easily bears his absence without venomous despair and over-painful bitterness.

- How sweet the name of Jesus sounds
  in a believer's ear!
  It soothes our sorrows, heals our wounds,
  and drives away our fear.
  It makes the wounded spirit whole

and calms the troubled breast;
'tis manna to the hungry soul,
and to the weary, rest. (John Newton, 1779)

32.

Bernard of Clairvaux on the Song of Songs 3:1

On my bed by night
I sought him whom my soul loves;
I sought him, but found him not.

Seeking God is not only something unbelievers do, says Bernard of Clairvaux (see #5); Christians should seek God as well. Finding joy in Christ means we want to go on finding joy in Christ. But Bernard also reminds us that we only seek God because He first sought us: 'We love because he first loved us' (1 John 4:19).

It is a great good to seek God. I think that, among all the blessings of the soul, there is none greater than this. It is the first of the gifts of God and the last goal of the soul's progress. No virtue precedes it, and none surpasses it. What could be better since nothing precedes it and what could surpass that which is the consummation of all other virtues? For what virtue can be ascribed to someone who is not seeking God, or what limit prescribed to one who is seeking him? 'Seek his presence continually' (Ps. 105:4), says the Psalmist.

I think that even when a soul has found God it will not stop seeking him. For God is sought, not by the movement of the feet, but by the desires of the heart. And when a soul has enjoyed the happiness of finding him, that sacred desire is not extinguished. On the contrary, it is increased. Is the consummation of the joy the extinction of the desire? It is instead like oil poured on a fire; for desire is, as it were, aflame. Yes, this is indeed the case.

The joy will be fulfilled, but its fulfilment is not the end of desire, and therefore it is not the end of seeking. Do not think love earnestly seeks God because he is absent and do not think that a desire for him arises from anxiety. His constant presence excludes the former, and the abundance of his grace prevents the latter.

But observe now why I have said this. It is so that every soul among you which seeks God should know that you seek him because he first sought you. Your soul has been sought by God before it began to seek him. If we are not aware of this, then a great blessing might cause great harm. This harm occurs when, having been filled with the good gifts from the Lord, a soul treats those gifts as if they had *not* been received from God, and so does not glorify God for them. There is no doubt that in this way those who appeared great in human eyes because of the graces conferred on them, were in fact counted as the least before God. For they did not glorify God ... He who is the best of men may become the worst in this way. For without doubt, if someone claims the credit for their excellence, then such a person becomes blameworthy instead of praiseworthy.

'On my bed I sought him whom my soul loves.' The soul seeks the Word, but it had been first sought by the Word. Otherwise, once it had been cast out of the presence of the Word, it would not have returned to see the good things. It only returned because it had first been sought by the Word ...

'I sought him,' says the Bride, 'him whom my soul loves.' It is that you might seek him that God in his goodness seeks you and loves you first. It is to this that his goodness is calling you and arousing you. You would not seek him at all, O soul, nor love him at all, if you had not been first sought and first loved. You have been pre-empted by a twofold blessing: that of love and that of seeking. The love is the cause of the seeking; and the seeking is the fruit and the proof of the love. You have been loved so that you need not fear you were being sought so you could be punished. And you were sought so that you might not complain you were loved in vain. Each of these two great and unmistakable favours gives you courage. Each has removed your shyness, touched your feelings, and moved you to return. This is the reason for any zeal and ardour that moves us to seek him whom our soul loves. Just as you were not able to seek him until you had first been sought, so now that you have been sought, you are unable to do anything other than seek him.

• 'God is sought not on foot but by desire.'

33.

James Durham on the Song of Songs 3:2-3

I will rise now and go about the city,
in the streets and in the squares;
I will seek him whom my soul loves.
I sought him, but found him not.
The watchmen found me
as they went about in the city.
'Have you seen him whom my soul loves?'

James Durham (see #13) says the 'watchmen' represent church ministers. Minsters defend Christ's people by watching out for straying sheep and fierce wolves (false teachers). Durham says the watchmen 'found' the bride as their teaching brought conviction to her heart, even though they themselves may have been unaware of her circumstances.

The minister's office is implied here. This city has watchmen which is what ministers are called (Ezek. 3:17. Isa. 62:6. Heb. 13:17). The word implies that the church is a city in danger, having outward and inward enemies, and therefore in need of watchmen. Therefore ministers are appointed in the church to guard against, and prevent, the dangers it faces. Some are specifically designed, and set apart from others, for this purpose. This office is necessary, burdensome, and of great importance for the safety of the church, just as watchmen are to a city. For ministers watch over the souls of the people committed to their trust. Here we see that these watchmen are exercising their duty, for 'they went about the city'. This shows their diligence in guarding what is entrusted to them, and sets out the end for which they are appointed ...

These watchmen found her. I take this to mean that by their teaching they spoke to her condition. By their searching and particular application of their preaching and counsel, they made the two-edged sword of God's word reach her. It was as if they had spoken specifically to her, beyond all the rest of the congregation. This shows the effectiveness of God's word when rightly managed. It is a discerner of the thoughts and intents of the heart (Heb. 4:12). God can make it find out one in the midst of many others, without the minister knowing their circumstances. God can make it speak to a believer's case, or any other particular person's condition, as if the preacher knew and aimed his application specifically at them. So ministers should be looking for the different ways their teaching applies to a variety of conditions. They ought to differentiate between the precious and the vile, and rightly divide the word of truth ...

Ministers are suitable physicians of the soul (though not the sole or only physician) to whom believers can reveal what is exercising their soul. And, therefore, there should be much spiritual sympathy between them and their people. It's a great encouragement to a distressed soul to impart its case to a minister when God has used his public teaching to speak pertinently to it.

- Pray that Christ would use the preaching of your church to speak to the needs of your heart.

34.

Charles Spurgeon on the Song of Songs 3:4

Scarcely had I passed them
when I found him whom my soul loves.
I held him, and would not let him go

Charles Spurgeon (see #7) says we hold Christ (i.e. maintain our experience of Him) by resolve and faith. Spurgeon gives us model prayers to help us do this. But, just as Bernard said, we seek Christ because He first sought us (see #32), so Spurgeon says we hold on to Christ because He enables us to hold on to Him. We could never keep the all-powerful God in our grip without the all-powerful God strengthening our grip!

How are we to hold Christ? Well, first, let us hold him by our heart's resolve, and it shall be as chains of gold to fasten him to you. Say to him:

'My Lord, will you go away from me? See how happy you have made me. A glimpse of your love has made me so blest that I do not envy the angels before your throne. Will you take that joy away from me by taking yourself away? Why did you give me a taste of your love if you did not mean to give me more? You have spoilt me now for all my former joy. O stay with me, my Master, or else I will be unhappy indeed! Lord, if you go, your chosen one will be unsafe. There is a wolf prowling about. What will your poor lamb do without you, O mighty Shepherd? Will you deliver your turtle-dove over to the cruel fowler who seeks to slay her? Therefore, abide with me.'

As long as you can find arguments for his staying, Christ does not want to go from you. His delights are with the children of men, and he is happy in the company of those whom he has purchased with his precious blood ... Be bold enough even to say to him, 'I will not let you go unless you bless me' (Gen. 32:26). Let each of us cry, 'Christ for me! Go, harlot-world. Do not come near even the outside of my door. Go away, for my heart is with my Lord, and he is my soul's chief treasure.'

Hold him, too, with a simple faith. That is a wonderful hold-fast. Say to him:

> 'My Lord, I have found you now, and I rejoice in you. But even if you hide your face from me, I will still believe in you. If I never see a smile from you again till I see you on your throne, yet I will not doubt you, for my heart is fixed, not so much upon the realisation of your presence, as upon yourself and your finished work. Though you slay me, yet will I hope in you (Job 13:15.')

And I, a poor trembling creature, may hold the Omnipotent himself, and say to him, 'I will not let you go.' How is that wonder to be accomplished? I will tell you. If Omnipotence helps you to hold Omnipotence, why, then, the deed is done! If Christ, and not you alone, holds Christ, then Christ is held indeed, for shall he vanquish his own self? No.

- Spurgeon continues: 'Master, you could slay death, and break the old serpent's head, but you cannot conquer your own self. And if you are in me, I can hold you, for it is not I, but Christ in me, that holds Christ, and will not let him go.'

35.

Charles Spurgeon on the Song of Songs 3:4-5

Scarcely had I passed them
when I found him whom my soul loves.
I held him, and would not let him go
until I had brought him into my mother's house,
and into the chamber of her who conceived me.
I adjure you, O daughters of Jerusalem,
by the gazelles or the does of the field,
that you not stir up or awaken love
until it pleases.

Charles Spurgeon (see #7) interprets 'my mother's house' as the church. The church's power, he says, lies in the presence of Christ. But that requires Christ to be the experience of the individual members of the church. So Spurgeon exhorts us to lay hold of Christ through faith and obedience, while also reminding us that Christ is willing to be held by those who truly seek Him.

The fact is that Christ Jesus is present in his church by the Holy Spirit ... As God, Jesus is everywhere; as man, he is only in heaven; as God and man in one person, Mediator and Head of the Church, he is present with us by the Holy Spirit, the Comforter, whom the Father has sent in his name ... This presence - not a bodily, but a spiritual presence - is the glory of the church of God. When she is without it, she is shorn of her strength; when she possesses it, all good things follow ...

We learn from the text that before ever we can bring the Beloved into our mother's house (the church), we must find him personally for ourselves ... These ardent lovers of Jesus must diligently seek him ... It may be our lax living, our neglect of prayer, or some other fault, that has taken from us the light of his countenance. Let us resolve today that there shall be no rest in our souls until once again he has returned to us in the fulness of his manifested love, and abides in our hearts. If any sin obstructs the way, it must be rigorously given up. If there is any neglected duty, it must be earnestly discharged. Sacrifices we must make and penalties we must endure, but to Christ we must come. For we are feeble when we are absent from him, and quite incapable of rendering any great service to the church till once for all we can say, 'I found him, I held him, and would not let him go' ...

I beg every believer ask themselves a few questions, such as these: 'Am I walking in constant fellowship with Christ? If I am not, why not? Is it that I am worldly, or proud, or indolent, or envious, or careless? Am I indulging myself in any sin? Is there anything whatever that divides me from Christ my Lord?' Let this be the resolution of every one of the Lord's people: 'From this time on, I will seek the Lord my Saviour, and I will not be satisfied until I can say, "I am coming up from the wilderness leaning upon the Beloved"' (Song 3:6).

But note, next, he is very willing to be held. Who could hold him if he were not? He is the omnipotent Saviour, and if he willed to withdraw he could do so ... He loves that sacred violence which takes him by force, that holy diligence which does not leave a gap open by which he may escape ... Jesus is willing enough to be retained by hearts which are full of his love ...

Now, then, hold him fast by your faith; trust him implicitly, rest in him for every day's cares. Hold him also with the grasp of love. Let your whole heart go out towards him. Embrace him with the arms of mighty affection, and enchain him with ardent admiration. Lay hold of him by faith, and clasp him with love.

Be also much in prayer. Prayer casts a chain about him. There is a sweet perfume about prayer that always attracts the Lord ...

Hold him, too, by your obedience to him. Never quarrel with him. Let him have his way. He will stay nowhere where some other will lord it over his own. Be very tender in your conduct, so that nothing will grieve him. Show him that you are ready to suffer for his sake.

I believe that where there is a prayerful, careful, holy, loving, believing walk towards Jesus, the fellowship of the saint with his Lord will not be broken and may continue for months and years.

- Am I walking in fellowship with Christ? If I am not, is it because I am worldly, proud, indolent, envious, or careless? Am I indulging in sin? Is there anything that divides me from Christ?

36.

George Swinnock on the Song of Songs 3:6-11

What is that coming up from the wilderness
like columns of smoke,
perfumed with myrrh and frankincense,
with all the fragrant powders of a merchant? ...
Go out, O daughters of Zion,
and look upon King Solomon ...
on the day of his wedding,
on the day of the gladness of his heart.

These verses describe the marriage procession, and marriage, of the bride and bridegroom. George Swinnock draws upon all the imagery of the Song of Songs to issue a marriage proposal, inviting us to join the bride of Christ in committing ourselves to Christ. In the days of arranged marriages, paintings were used to introduce potential suiters (just as today people use online dating profiles). Swinnock says the gospel message is God's picture to introduce us to Christ. Swinnock (1627-1673) was a Puritan minister in Hertfordshire and Buckinghamshire, England. He left the Church of England at the Great Ejection in 1662, and later became the pastor of a large nonconformist church in Kent.

For your eternal good, I have a special offer to make to you from the blessed God, and that is of a marriage with his only Son, the Lord Jesus Christ. I am this day sent to you, as his ambassador, with full instructions to woo on his behalf, that I might present you a chaste virgin to Christ. You need not doubt my authority, for in the Scriptures you may read my commission

111

and credential letters, which may give you full security and satisfaction against all jealousies and suspicions which can possibly arise in your breast. You need not question the reality of God's offer of so great a fortune to you, notwithstanding all your unworthiness. For he sent his Son on so great a journey, from heaven to earth, to marry your nature, so that he might be married to your person. And he caused him to pay an infinite cost to provide glorious attire, and precious jewels, out of heaven's wardrobe and cabinet, that you might be adorned as a fitting spouse of so great a Lord.

He himself has sent you his picture, of greater value than heaven and earth, drawn at length and to life in the gospel, in all his royalty, beauty, and glory so you can see whether you can like and love his person. Friend, look longingly on him, consider his person. He is fairer than any of the children of men. He is the exact image of his Father's person. Your beloved (oh, shall I call him so!) is pure and wholesome, the fairest of ten thousands. He is altogether lovely, and nothing but amiableness. None ever saw him without being enamoured with him.

View his inheritance: he is heir of all things; all power is given to him in heaven and earth. I know your poverty, but there are unsearchable riches in Christ, durable riches and righteousness. You are infinitely in debt, and thereby liable to the arrest of divine justice, and the eternal prison of hell. But I must tell you, the revenues of this emperor are able to discharge the debts of millions of worlds, and to leave enough, too, for their comfortable and honourable life throughout eternity.

Behold his parentage: he is the only-begotten of the Father, full of grace and truth, the eternal Son of God. As there is incomparable beauty and favour in his person, and inestimable riches and treasure in his portion; so there is unconceivable dignity and honour in his parentage. For he is the only natural Son and heir of the most high God. For your further awakening, he is your near kinsman, bone of your bone, and flesh of your flesh, and so has a right to you. God has given his stewards a

112

command, as Abraham his servant (Gen. 24:2-4), not to take a wife to his Son of the daughters of the Canaanites, from among the evil angels, but to go to his Son's own country and kindred, and to take a wife for him among the children of men.

Friend, you have heard the errand about which I am sent to you. I hope there is such an arrow of love darted into your heart from the gracious eyes and looks of this Lord of glory, that you are wounded, and begin to be taken with him, and to wish, 'Oh that I might have the honour and happiness to become the bride of so lovely a bridegroom, that this king of saints would take me, a poor sinner, into his bed and bosom.'

- Have you seen the picture of Christ presented in the gospel message? Will you say 'Yes' to Him today?

37.

Ambrose of Milan on the Song of Songs 3:6-11

What is that coming up from the wilderness
like columns of smoke,
perfumed with myrrh and frankincense,
with all the fragrant powders of a merchant? ...
King Solomon made himself a carriage
from the wood of Lebanon ...
Go out, O daughters of Zion,
and look upon King Solomon,
with the crown with which his mother crowned him
on the day of his wedding,
on the day of the gladness of his heart.

St Ambrose (c. 339 - c. 397) says the column of smoke represents the prayers of God's people, which are pleasing to God, and Solomon's carriage represents the merits of Christ, which bring rest to souls wearied through attempts at self-righteousness. These verses invite us to look upon Christ, who is the loving King and Husband of His people.

Seeing the Bride cleaving to Christ, then, and still ascending with him – for he stoops to meet and assist those who seek him repeatedly, that he may lift them up – the daughters of Jerusalem say, 'What woman is this coming up from the wilderness?' This earthly place of ours appears to be an uncultivated wilderness, filled with the brambles and thorns of our sins, and so they plainly wonder how a soul, which had earlier been left in that lower place, may cleave to God's Word and ascend after the manner of the shoot of a vine that climbs upward, like smoke that is created by a fire and seeks the heights, and then radiates a delightful fragrance. That fragrance, moreover, gives off the sweet aroma of reverent prayer, which like incense is directed in the sight of God. Further, we read in the Apocalypse that 'the smoke of the incense rose with the prayers of the saints' (Rev. 8:4), and this incense – that is, the prayers of the saints – is borne by an angel 'upon the golden altar before the throne' (Rev. 8:3) and gives off the sweet perfume, as it were, of reverent prayer, because it is compounded [made up] of prayer that asks not for corporeal things, but for things eternal and invisible. More than anything else, however, it gives off the fragrance of myrrh and frankincense because the soul has died to sin and lives to God.

Seeing the Bride ascending, therefore, and not holding back, and delighted by the fragrance of her merits – and what is more, recognizing that she is the Bride of that peace-bearing Solomon – they follow her in an ardent band right up to *Solomon's litter*, because true rest in Christ is owed her. For Christ is the bed of the saints, upon whom the weary hearts of every one of them rest from the struggles of this age ...

Once the Bride has been brought to the rest that belongs to the Bridegroom, therefore, they sing a wedding song, and say, 'Love from the daughters of Zion. Come forth and behold King Solomon with the crown with which his mother crowned him, on the day of his wedding.' They are singing an epithalamium [a marriage song], and they are calling on the rest of the heavenly powers, or the souls, to see the love that Christ has with regard to the daughters of Jerusalem. That is why he deserved to be crowned by his mother as Son of love, even as Paul shows when he says, 'He has delivered us from the domain of darkness and transferred us to the kingdom of his Son of love' (Col. 1:13). Therefore he is Son of love and is himself love, not being accidentally possessed of love, but possessing it forever in what he is, just as he possesses the kingdom of which he said, 'For this purpose I was born' (John 18:37). That is why they say, 'Come forth,' that is, 'Come away from the cares and thoughts of this age, come away from bodily constraints, come away from the vanities of the world – and behold what love the peace-bearing King has on the day of his wedding, how glorious he is, because he gives resurrection to bodies and joins souls to himself. This is the victor's crown of the great contest, this is the magnificent wedding-present of Christ, his blood and his suffering.'

- Ambrose continues: 'For what more could he give, who did not hold himself back, but offered his death for our benefit?'

38.

James Durham on the Song of Songs 3:7-8

Behold, it is the litter of Solomon!
Around it are sixty mighty men,
some of the mighty men of Israel,
all of them wearing swords
and expert in war,
each with his sword at his thigh,
against terror by night.

James Durham (see #13) says the mighty men who protect the marriage procession are angels. But Durham's focus is on Christ: it is Christ who guards us 'against terror by night' (sometimes through angels). Christians can experience dark times of doubt and fear. But we are better protected, says Durham, than any earthly ruler. And Christ will ensure we make it safely home to glory with Him.

'By night' here is understood the darkness, so to speak, faced by believers in which fears, doubts, challenges and so on are ready to assault them, like attacks befall people in the night. These words show the role that our Solomon, Jesus, has in guarding his people, to quieten us against the doubtings, difficulties, discouragements, and the like that believers are so subject in their drooping, night-time conditions. For when light shines, they are little troubled.

These words show that Christ's Bride, admitted to fellowship with him, may still have her dark nights. Believers, who have thought themselves above doubt and fear when things went well with them, may yet in nights of temptation, darkness and trial be overtaken with many sad fears. It's not always day with them, and when it's night with them, they are prone to fear.

Yet believers in their night-time experiences, when they are under their fears, have good security and an excellent guard. Indeed, their safety and defence is as good then as when there is no night, nor fear. However dark their night may be, Christ's protection is sufficient to preserve them. Christ is tender even of believers' fears, and has provided for their peace. He has appointed means not only to prevent their hurt, but also to prevent their fears. For, because of fear, he has appointed this guard.

There is no King or Monarch so well attended and guarded, or who may sleep so secure and sound, as a believer. His guard is still at their post, and they are valiant men who cannot fail. For he is at peace with God, and he that is within the peace of God has the warrant, right and advantage of it to guard his heart and mind (Phil. 4:7). The believer has all the promises, and confirmations of oath and seals in which it is impossible for God to lie, to secure and quiet him. The believer is watched over by angels (Ps. 34:7). Angels pitch their tents around him, and their chariots wait on him. And believers have God himself, and his almighty power for their defence, who alone may make them dwell in safety, so that they may lie down with confidence, and quietly sleep (Ps. 4:8). It's good sleeping in Christ's bed – there is not so good a rest to be found anywhere in the world.

So then by this guard is understood whatever contributes to confirm the faith of believers, and strengthen them against their fears of being interrupted in their rest, which (being in Christ) is available to them.

- What might it mean for you today to rest on the promises of Christ?

39.

Charles Spurgeon on the Song of Songs 3:9-10

King Solomon made himself a carriage;
from the wood of Lebanon.
He made its posts of silver,
its back of gold, its seat of purple;
its interior was inlaid with love
by the daughters of Jerusalem.

Just as Solomon sent his carriage to carry his bride to their wedding, so Christ carries His people safely to our wedding with Him in glory. Charles Spurgeon (see #7) shows how Christ ensures our safe passage by using the image of the carriage to show how the different attributes of God reinforce the effectiveness of Christ's atoning work.

This palanquin (or travelling chariot) in which the king is carried represents the covenant of grace, the plan of salvation, by which Jesus bears his people through the wilderness of this world, onward to the rest which he has prepared for them. It is in a word the mediatorial work of Jesus. The ark was carried through the wilderness preceded by the pillar of cloud and fire, as a symbol of the divine presence in mercy, and here we have a similar representation of the great King of grace, borne in regal splendour through the world, and bearing his elect spouse with him ...

As for the silver pillars which bear up the canopy, to what should I liken them but to the attributes of God which support and guarantee the effectiveness of the great atonement of Christ, beneath which we are sheltered?

- There is the silver pillar of God's justice. He cannot smite the soul that hides beneath the cross of Christ. If Christ has paid the debt, how is it possible that God should visit again a second time the iniquity of his people, first on their Surety, and then again on themselves?

- Then stands next the solid pillar of his power. 'They will never perish, and no one will snatch them out of my hand. My Father, who has given them to me, is greater than all, and no one is able to snatch them out of the Father's hand' (John 10:28-29).

- Then on the other side is the pillar of his love, a silver pillar indeed, bright and sparkling to the eye – love unchanging and eternal, strong as the power of, and fast as, the justice which bears up the canopy on the other side.

- And here, on this side, stands immutability, another column upon which the atonement rests. If God could change, then he might cast away his blood-bought people. But because 'I the Lord do not change; therefore you, O children of Jacob, are not consumed' (Mal. 3:6).

- The covering of the chariot is purple. Look up, Christian, and delight yourself in that blood-red canopy which shelters you. From hell and heaven, from time and eternity, you are secured by this covering ...

- As for the bottom of this palanquin, which is of gold – may not this represent the eternal purpose and counsel of God, that purpose which he formed in himself before ever the earth existed? I do not know, brothers and sisters, how it is with you, but I find it most pleasant to have as the basis of my hope, the firm decree of God. Atonement covers me, I know, but still on this I must rest: God decrees it, he has said it, and it must be done; he has commanded and it stands fast ...

So come and sit side-by-side with Jesus in his chariot of grace, his bed of rest. Come and recline with him in holy fellowship. There is room enough for you, and strength enough to bear your weight.

- Jesus said: 'Come to me, all who labour and are heavy laden, and I will give you rest' (Matt. 11:28).

40.

Alexander Moody Stuart on the Song of Songs 4:1-7

Behold, you are beautiful, my love,
behold, you are beautiful! ...
You are altogether beautiful, my love;
there is no flaw in you.

In these verses, Christ celebrates the beauty of His bride. Alexander Moody Stuart (see #10) shows us a before-and-after picture of believers: before we knew Christ our sin made us ugly; but now, through Christ, we are beautiful. We are *already beautiful* because we are righteous in Christ, and we are *becoming beautiful* because the Holy Spirit is making us more like Christ.

'From the sole of the foot even to the head, there is no soundness in it, but bruises and sores and raw wounds' (Isa. 1:6). Such is the believer by nature. 'You are altogether beautiful, my love; there is no flaw in you' (Song 4:7). Such is the same believer through grace. The church in herself, in all her features and in all her members, is to the Lord Jesus an object of highest esteem for her worth, of intense admiration for her beauty, and of most ardent love for her exceeding loveliness. She was guilty, vile, useless, but 'Christ loved the church and gave himself up for her, that he might sanctify her, having cleansed her by the washing of water with the word' (Eph. 5:25-26). He looked on the unlovely with inconceivable compassion 'because of the great love with which he loved us even when we were dead in our trespasses' (Eph. 2:4-5). But he so loved us as to secure us through his own blood, that the church should forever be distinguished by her own loveliness, even as she had been distinguished by being his beloved ... The church's beauty, defective and marred, is made 'perfect through the splendour that [the Lord GOD] bestowed on [her]' (Ezek. 16:14).

The Bride of the Lamb is invested with a double beauty: with the beauty of the Lord her God upon her and with the beauty of holiness within her; by Christ clothing her with righteousness all glorious around and by the Spirit creating her anew, 'all glorious within' (Ps. 45:13 KJV). In the beauty of Jesus the soul is lovely in the hour of its acceptance. Of the criminals pardoned but yesterday Jesus declares: 'The glory that you have given me I have given to them' (John 17:22). To the sinner newly-washed Jesus announces: 'already you are clean because of the word that I have spoken to you' (John 15:3). 'You are altogether beautiful, my love; there is no flaw in you' (Song 4:7). This beauty does not change. It is never enhanced, and it is never impaired ... It is all fair, and always fair; without blemish and incapable of blemish. It is as fair and spotless on the guiltiest transgressor in earth as on the Apostle Paul in heaven, being 'found in [Christ], not having a righteousness of my own that comes from the law, but that which comes through faith in Christ' (Phil. 3:9).

Simultaneously with the imputation of justifying righteousness, and the sprinkling of cleansing blood is the formation of a new creation by the Spirit, in child-like resemblance to the Father, in brother-like similarity to his first-born Son ... The new creature, 'born of God' and who 'does not keep on sinning' (1 John 5:18), is the fair handiwork of Jehovah, and like all his works is 'very good' (Gen. 1:31).

But it is encumbered with the body of sin and death, marring its beauty, chaining its energies, hindering its growth. Its beauty, therefore, varies according to whether it is seen in its heavenly beauty, thriving in the midst of all the obstructions of earth and hell, or whether it is found feeble in its own energies, oppressed by Satan and spattered by the world. 'You are altogether beautiful, my love,' is never withheld by Christ from the believing soul.

For he not only says to his disciples, 'already you are clean because of the word that I have spoken to you' (John 15:3), but even when men would have judged otherwise, he says of them 'they have your word' (John 17:6).

But it is when they 'walk in a manner worthy of the Lord, fully pleasing to him' (Col. 1:10) that the satisfaction of the Lord Jesus over his people is full. Then his joy in them remains, and his heart freely declares: 'Behold, you are beautiful, my love, behold, you are beautiful!'

- You may frown as you see your sin. But Christ smiles as He sees His beauty in you.

41.

Thomas Boston on the Song of Songs 4:8

Come with me from Lebanon, my bride;
come with me from Lebanon.
Depart from the peak of Amana,
from the peak of Senir and Hermon,
from the dens of lions,
from the mountains of leopards.

Thomas Boston (see #17) interprets this call to come from the mountains as a call to turn away from worldliness. The world (in the sense of human culture in opposition to God) may appear pleasant, but it is spiritually dangerous. But this is simply a call to give up pleasure because Christ is 'a better place' to be, a place that brings greater satisfaction.

Verse 8 describes Christ's gracious call to his people to leave the world as mountains of vanity. The world's glory dazzles the eyes, and arrests the hearts, even of the Lord's people, till they see the transcendent glory of their Lord. This vision of glory looses them from the hold of the world, and makes them willing to go to Christ rather than to sit in the world's embraces. Christ's gracious call is to leave the world as mountains of prey, dangerous mountains. It is likely all these mountains were pleasant ones. But they were dangerous, for the lions had their dens there and the leopards their haunts. And thus the world is a dangerous place to Christ's spouse. She is in danger while in it. Even in the midst of worldly joy, there are fearful snares.

The lions' dens are expressed emphatically to strike her with a horror of the place, that she may haste away ...

There is a natural coming out of it through death when we bid farewell forever to the deceitful world. But there is also a spiritual coming out of it, namely, in heart and affection (Matt. 6:20). Thus believers in the exercise of grace are making their way out of it. They are coming up from the wilderness leaning upon their beloved. Though they are in the world, yet they live like people of another world. Though their bodies are on the earth, yet their hearts are in heaven. This is what Christ is calling you to this day ...

Turn your backs then upon the things of the world. Be mortified to them (Gal. 6:14). Our hearts are naturally glued to the world. Now let the bond be loosed at Christ's call, that you may mount upwards. The smiling world is meeting and embracing some. It is casting into their lap plentifully, and they have the prospect of more. But oh take heed to the dangerous embraces of the world, lest it hug you to death, as surely it will, if you do not shake yourselves loose of it ...

Our Lord has a better place for your reception than the world can be in its best dress (Heb. 11:16). It is the better country, Immanuel's land, the land that is blessed with an eternal spring, in which are no clouds, no night, but an eternal day. If you enquire about the profits of the house, there is in it an eternal weight of glory ...

Our Lord displays his glory to you in the gospel, to win your hearts and get you to come away with him. 'Come,' says he, 'with me.' It is as if he had said, 'Looking to me will cure the madness and frenzy into which looking at the bewitching world has cast you.' When the sun appears, the stars hide their heads, and have no beauty in comparison; so the glory of the Son of God, discerned by faith, will make all the glory of the world look like a small candle in the sunlight, going out with smoke ... In the enjoyment of Christ, you will not be grieved with disappointments as you have been from the world ... He will satisfy the desires of your hearts, which the world never could and never shall satisfy.

- Fading is the worldling's pleasure,
  all his boasted pomp and show.
  Solid joys and lasting treasure
  none but Zion's children know. (John Newton, 1779)

42.

Richard Sibbes on the Song of Songs 4:9

You have captivated my heart, my sister, my bride;

Richard Sibbes (see #2) says we are Christ's *sister* in the sense that Christ and His people share the same human nature, as a result of the incarnation. And the church is Christ's *bride* because it has come from His wounded side, just as Eve was formed from Adam's side. But a marriage always requires consent, and it is the Holy Spirit who wins our heart so that we consent to our marriage to Christ. Just as a wife takes her husband's surname, so we take Christ's name with all the privileges it brings.

'My sister, my bride.' It is a point of comfort to know that we have a brother who is a favourite in heaven. Unless he had been our brother, he could not have been our husband; for husband and wife should be of one nature. That he might marry us, therefore, he came and took our nature. But now he is in heaven, sat down at the right hand of God. What a comfort it is to a poor soul that has no friends in the world to know that they have a friend in heaven who will acknowledge them as his brother or sister ... The church is the daughter of a King, born of God, the sister and spouse of a King, because she is the sister and spouse of Christ, and the mother of all who are spiritual kings. The church of Christ is royal in every way. Therefore we are kings because we are Christians.

The church is also the spouse of Christ. It springs out of him. Just as Eve was taken out of Adam's rib, so the spouse of Christ was taken out of his side. When his side was pierced, the church rose out of his blood. For he redeemed it, by satisfying divine justice ...

Again, another foundation of this marriage between Christ and us is that he works in us by his Spirit so that we yield to him. There must be consent on our part and this is not in us by nature. But it has been won by his Spirit. We yield to take him upon his own terms, that is, that we should leave our father's house, all our former fleshly commitments, when he has won our consent. Then the marriage between him and us is struck ...

In a human marriage the husband takes his wife under his own name. She, losing her own name, is called by his. In the same way, we are called 'Christians', those who belong to Christ. In a human marriage the wife is received with all her debts, and becomes sharer in the honours and riches of her husband. Whatever he has is hers, and he stands answerable for all her debts. So it is here: we have not only the name of Christ upon us, but we share his honours. There is a blessed exchange between Christ and us. His honours and riches are ours. Meanwhile, we have nothing to bestow on him, but our poverty, sins and miseries, which he took upon him ...

Let us often think of the connection between Christ and us, if we have given our names to him, and so let us not be discouraged by any sin or unworthiness in us. For who sues a wife for debt when she is married? Therefore answer all accusations thus: 'Go to Christ. If you have anything to say to me, go to my husband.' God is just, and he will not have his justice twice satisfied, and whatever is due has already been satisfied by Christ our husband. What a comfort this is to a distressed conscience! If sin – which is the ill of ills and cause of all evil – cannot dismay us, what other ill can dismay us? He that exhorts us to bear with the infirmities one of another, and has exhorted the husband to bear with the wife as the weaker vessel (1 Pet. 3:7), will not he bear with his church as the weaker vessel, performing the duty of an husband in all our infirmities?

- If Satan accuses you or fears torment you, say: 'Go to Christ. If you have anything to say to me, go to my husband.'

43.

Matthew Henry on the Song of Songs 4:9

You have captivated my heart, my sister, my bride;
you have captivated my heart with one glance of your eyes,
with one jewel of your necklace.

Christ does not speak empty words of love, says Matthew
Henry (see #20), for he demonstrated the depth of His love by
dying for His bride. His love was 'mindless': not in the sense
of bring foolish, but in the sense of not minding the cost.

We see here the great delight Christ takes in his church and
in all believers. He delights in them as in an agreeable bride,
'adorned for her husband' (Rev. 21.2), who greatly desires her
beauty (Ps. 45:11). No expressions of love can be more passionate
than those here, in which Christ manifests his affection to his
church. And yet that great proof of his love, his dying for us
that he might present us to himself as a glorious church, goes far
beyond them all. A spouse so dearly paid for and bought could
not but be dearly loved. Such a price being given for her, a high
value must accordingly be put upon her. And both together may
well set us a wondering at 'the breadth and length and height
and depth' of the 'the love of Christ that surpasses knowledge'
(Eph. 3:18-19), that love through which he gave himself for us
and gives himself to us.

Observe, how he is affected towards his spouse: 'You have
captivated my heart.' The word is only used here. It means, 'You
have hearted me,' or 'You have unhearted me.' New words are
coined to express the inexpressible nature of Christ's surprising

love to his church. And the strength of that love is set forth by that which is considered a weakness in men, namely being so much in love with one object as to be heartless towards everything else ... Christ's heart is upon his church - so it has appeared all along. His treasure is in it; it is his 'treasured possession' (Exod. 19:5). Bishop Reynolds says: 'Never was love like unto the love of Christ, which made him even mindless of himself, when he emptied himself of his glory, and despised all shame and pain, for our sakes. The wound of love towards us, which he had from eternity in himself, made him neglect all the wounds and reproaches of the cross.' Thus let us love him.

• Christ's love for us so captivated His thoughts that He gave no thought for Himself, but instead offered Himself on the cross for us.

44.

Robert Murray M'Cheyne on the Song of Songs 4:10

How beautiful is your love, my sister, my bride!

Robert Murray M'Cheyne (see #22) says being Christ's sister and bride must go together. Some people want to be His spouse (being loved by Him) without being His sister (living like Him). Other people get the order wrong and try to be Christ's sister (living like Him) so that they can become His spouse (being loved by Him). But His love always comes first. We can only obey Him when our hearts have been won by His love. And we can only be *like* Him by first being joined *to* Him.

There are many sweet names from the lips of Christ addressed to believers ... But here is one more tender than all, 'My sister, my bride' in verse 9, and again in verse 10 and in verse 12 – a *wife* by covenant, a *sister* by being born of the same Father in heaven. To be spoken well of by the world is little to be desired; but to hear Christ speak such words to us is enough to fill our hearts with heavenly joy ...

These two things are inseparable. Some would like to be *the spouse* of the Saviour, without being the sister – to be saved by Christ, but not to be made like Christ. When Christ chooses a sinner, and sets his love on the soul, and when he woos the soul and draws it into covenant with himself, it is only that he may make the soul a sister, that he may impart his features, his same heart, his all, to the soul. Now, many rest in the mere forgiveness of sins. Many have felt Christ wooing their soul, and offering himself freely to them, and they have accepted him. They have consented to the match and their heart is filled with joy in being taken into covenant with so glorious a bridegroom. But why has he done it? To make you a partaker of his holiness, to change your nature, to make you a sister to himself – of his own mind and spirit.

You cannot be the spouse of Christ without also becoming sister. Christ offers to be the bridegroom of sin-covered souls. He came from heaven for this; took flesh and blood for this. He tries to woo sinners, ... telling them of all his power, and glory, and riches, and that all shall be theirs. He is a blood-sprinkled bridegroom, but that is his chief loveliness. The soul believes his word, melts under his love, consents to be his. 'My beloved is mine, and I am his.' Then he washes the soul in his own blood; clothes it in his own righteousness; takes it in with him to the presence of his Father.

From that day the soul begins to reflect his image. Christ begins to live in the soul. The same heart, the same spirit, are in both. The soul becomes sister as well as spouse – Christ's not only by choice and covenant, but also by likeness. Some of you Christ has chosen; you have become his justified ones. Do you rest there? No, remember you must be made like him, reflecting his image. You cannot separate the two.

Notice, also the order of the two: you must be first the spouse before you can be the sister of Christ. You must be his by covenant before you can be his by likeness. Some think to be like Christ first, thinking they will copy his features till they recommend themselves to Christ. No, this will not do. He chooses only those that have no beauty, polluted in their own blood, that he may have the honour of washing them. 'When I passed by you and saw you wallowing in your blood, I said to you in your blood, "Live!"' (Ezek. 16:6). Are there any trying to recommend themselves to Christ by their change of life? Oh, how little you know him! He comes to seek those who are dark in themselves. Are there some of you who are poor, defiled, and unclean? You are just the kind of soul Christ woos. Proud and scornful? Christ woos you. He offers you his all – and then he will change you.

- What is your danger? To want to be loved by Christ without living like Christ? Or to try to be loved by Christ by living like Christ?

45.

Charles Spurgeon on the Song of Songs 4:10

How beautiful is your love, my sister, my bride!
How much better is your love than wine,
and the fragrance of your oils than any spice!

We are right to value Christ's love to us. But, says Charles
Spurgeon (see #7), we also need to see how much Christ values
our love to Him, however inconsistent our love may be. Christ
does not despise our faith, hope, patience, and humility, even
though they are often weak, feeble, and faltering. He treasures
these things, and they bring Him pleasure. When we speak to
one another of Christ's goodness or when we pray on our own,
Christ, as it were, is in the room, delighting in what He sees.

Hearken to what the Lord Jesus says to you today by his Holy
Spirit from this song! Your love – poor, feeble, and cold though
it be – is very precious to the Lord Jesus. You value his love,
and you are right in doing so. But I am afraid that you still
undervalue it. He even values your love and, if I may so speak,
he sets a far higher estimate upon it than you do. He thinks
very much of little, estimating it not by its strength, but by its
sincerity. 'Ah,' he says, 'they do love me, they do love me, I know
they do. They sin, they disobey me, but still I know they love
me. Their heart is true. They do not love me as I deserve, but
still they love me.' Jesus Christ is delighted with the thought
that his people love him, which cheers and gladdens him. Just
as the thought of his love gladdens us, so the thought of our
love gladdens him.

Notice how he puts it when he says, 'How much better is your love than wine!' Jesus Christ looks upon his people's love as being a luxury to him. When he sat at the feast of Simon the Pharisee in Luke 7, I have no doubt there were sparkling wine cups on the table, and many rich dainties. But Jesus Christ did not care for the wine or for the banquet. What did he care for? That poor woman's love which was much better to him than wine. I will go farther. When Christ went to his cross, there was one thing that cheered him even in the agonies of death; it was the thought of his people's love (Heb. 12:2).

Do not imagine that Christ despises our faith, or our hope, or our patience, or our humility. All these *graces* are precious to him, and they are described in the next sentence under the title of ointment. The working of these graces, their exercise and development, are compared with the smell of ointment ...

'I confess,' say you, 'I cannot look on my graces with any pride. I can only weep over them, for they are so marred by my own evil nature.' But now then, the very things that you and I very properly weep over, Christ delights in. He loves all these. The smell may seem to be only very faint and feeble, yet Jesus observes it, Jesus smells it, Jesus loves it, and Jesus approves it.

O Jesus, this is condescension indeed, to be pleased with such poor things as we display. Oh, this is love, and proves your love to us, that you can make so much out of so little, and esteem so highly that which is of such little worth!

Have you never known a little child when he feels love in his heart go into the garden or the field and bring you a little flower. It may be only a little buttercup or daisy, a great thing to him, perhaps, but a trifle to you, worthless in fact. Yet you took it and smiled and felt happy because it was a token of your child's love? Such is Christ's attitude to your love.

Sometimes believers are privileged to sit down together, and speak of Christ's exceeding glories and his boundless love. Do you know that Jesus is in that room? Smiling, Jesus is there. And he is saying to his own soul, 'It is good to be here; the lips of these brothers and sisters drip nectar and their words are sweet to me.' At another time the Christian is alone in his room, and talks with his God in a few broken words, and with many sighs, many tears, and many groans. Little does he realise that Jesus Christ is there, saying to such a one, 'Your lips drip nectar, my bride, honey and milk are under your tongue.'

- When it comes to the obedience of His people, Christ 'thinks very much of little.'

46.

Richard of Saint Victor on the Song of Songs 4:11

Your lips drip nectar, my bride;
honey and milk are under your tongue;
the fragrance of your garments is like the fragrance of Lebanon.

Richard of Saint Victor says the lips of believers drip honey when we share encouraging words with people. We find these words in the Bible, and especially in what the Bible reveals of Christ. So when we read the Scriptures we are like bees gathering nectar. Richard (d. 1173) is thought to have been born in Scotland. He was prior of the Abbey of Saint Victor in Paris, and one of the most influential theologians and spiritual writers of the late middle ages.

It is the lips of the dedicated soul that are a 'dripping honeycomb', since they pour out liquid sweetness, and produce this for the edification of others. This honey the soul gathers from the manifold flowers of the Scripture. It searches for these flowers, it dwells upon them, from them it extracts and elicits the sweetness of spiritual delight. It disdains and sets aside the knowledge that puffs up; rather, it seeks after edification and chooses ideas for their delightful fragrance, not for their pretentious eloquence. It seeks out the examples provided by the saints and mentally picks them over; for they were flowers and bloomed like the palm tree. Just as their way of life was holy, so too were their words and teachings sweet and pleasant. The soul flies to flowers of this sort, and from them it gathers spiritual honey.

But especially [the soul gathers nectar] from that matchless flower, the flower that sprouted from the rod of Jesse [the Lord Jesus] ... in which there dwells the 'fulness' of Deity (cf. Col. 1:19), in whom are 'all the treasures of wisdom and knowledge' (Col. 2:3), in whom all the righteous bloom, and in whom they bear fruit both in the form of a good life and in holy knowledge ...

To this blooming and abundant field the Bride, like the prudent bee, makes her way. She runs to the fragrance of this flower. She pursues him full of desire. By her love and her faith she attaches herself to him. From him, by the importunity of her prayer, she sucks the honey of grace. From his fulness she receives grace (cf. John 1:16). Charity is shed abroad in her heart by his Spirit (Rom. 5:5) ... Upon her lips, moreover, this grace is diffused, so that she gives off the fragrance of a heavenly sweetness to others.

She also has 'honey and milk under' her 'tongue', which is to say, refreshment for the strong, and for the faltering, encouragement: the solid food of the perfect [mature] and the milk of the simple teaching that is proper to those who are weak [Heb. 5:12-14]. For she has tasted the delight of the life to come ahead of time – the life in which souls are refreshed by the enjoyment of Christ's divinity and by the milk of his humanity. She has had a preliminary taste of that blessedness ... and this delight, like the current of a river, gives joy to the heavenly city of God, and it visits the little brooks, pilgrims and exiles on earth, to fill them gently and to renew them.

- Is there a word of encouragement from the Song of Songs that you could share with someone today?

47.

J. C. Ryle on the Song of Songs 4:12

A garden locked is my sister, my bride,
a spring locked, a fountain sealed.

What makes the church a garden separate from the world, says J. C. Ryle, is the eternal choice of the Father, the saving love of the Son, and regenerating work of the Spirit. It is this 'threefold work' that keeps us safe. J. C. Ryle (1816-1900) was an evangelical bishop in the Church of England and the first Bishop of Liverpool.

The Lord's garden has a distinctive peculiarity about it: it is a garden enclosed. There is an enclosure round believers ...

They are enclosed by God the Father's everlasting election. Long before they were born, long before the foundations of the world, God knew them, chose them, and appointed them to obtain salvation by Jesus Christ. The children of this world do not like to hear this doctrine proclaimed. It humbles people, and leaves no room to boast. But whether it is abused or not, the doctrine of election is true. It is the cornerstone of the believer's foundation, that we were chosen in Christ before the world began. Who can rightly estimate the strength of this enclosure?

They are enclosed by the special love of God the Son. The Lord Jesus is the Saviour of all men, but he is especially the Saviour of those who believe. He has power over all flesh, but he gives eternal life to those who are especially given to him, in a way that he does to no others. He shed his blood on the cross for all, but he only washes those who have a share in him. He invites all, but he quickens whom he will, and brings them to glory. He prays for them: he prays not for the world (John 17:9). He intercedes for them, that they may be kept from evil, that they may be sanctified by the truth, that their faith fail not (John 17:15-17). Who can fully describe the blessedness of this enclosure?

They are enclosed by the effective work of God the Holy Spirit. The Spirit of Christ calls them out from the world, and separates them as effectually as if a wall were built between them and it. He puts in them new hearts, new minds, new tastes, new desires, new sorrows, new joys, new wishes, new pleasures, new longings. He gives them new eyes, new ears, new affections, new opinions. He makes them new creatures; they are born again, and with a new birth they begin a new existence. Mighty indeed is the transforming power of the Holy Spirit! The believer and the world are completely put asunder, and everlastingly separated. You may place a believer and an unbeliever together, marry them, join them under one roof, but you cannot unite them any more into one piece. The one is part of the 'garden enclosed', and the other is not. Effectual calling is a barrier that cannot be broken.

Who can tell the comfort of this threefold wall of enclosure! Believers are enclosed by election, enclosed by washing and intercession, enclosed by calling and regeneration. Great is the consolation of these threefold bands of love around us, the love of God the Father, the love of God the Son, the love of God the Holy Spirit! ...

Blessed be God for this, that we are 'a garden enclosed!' Blessed be God. Our final safety hangs not on anything of our own – not on our graces and feelings, not on our degree of sanctification, not on our perseverance in doing good, not on our love, not on our growth in grace, not on our prayers and Bible-readings, not even on our faith. It hangs on nothing else but the work of Father, Son and Holy Spirit. If this threefold work enclose us, who shall overthrow our hope? If God be for us, who can be against us?

- 'A threefold cord is not quickly broken' (Eccl. 4:12).

48.

Charles Spurgeon on the Song of Songs 4:12

A garden locked is my sister, my bride,
a spring locked, a fountain sealed.

A garden, says Charles Spurgeon (see #7), is a piece of land separated from the wilderness around it. A Christian is like a garden in the sense that he is separate from the world around him. Indeed, the church will only be a blessing *to* the world by being different *from* the world. But we need to be different in the right way, says Spurgeon – not by living in a ghetto, but by being caring, forgiving, gentle, and loving.

A garden is a plot of ground separated from the common waste for a special purpose: such is the church ... Great attempts have been made of late to make the church receive the world, and, wherever it has succeeded, it has led to the world swallowing up the church ...

Let us, however, take heed that our separation from the world is of the same kind as our Lord's. We are not to adopt a peculiar dress, or a singular mode of speech, or shut ourselves out of society. He did not do so; for he was a man of the people, mixing with them for their good. He was seen at a wedding-feast aiding the festivities; he even ate in a Pharisee's house ... He did not exhibit any eccentricity of manner. He was separate from sinners only because he was holy and harmless, and they were not. He dwelt among us, for he was of us. No man was more a man than he; and yet, he was not of the world ...

We want all members of the church of Christ to be distinctive people, as much as if they were of a separate race, even when they are seen mingling with the people around them. We are not to cut ourselves off from our neighbours by affectation and contempt. God forbid! Our very avoiding of affectation, our naturalness, simplicity, sincerity, and amiability of character, should constitute our distinctiveness. Through Christians being what they seem to be, they should become remarkable in an age of pretenders. Their care for the welfare of others, their anxiety to do good, their forgiveness of injuries, their gentleness of manner – all these things should distinguish them far more than they could be distinguished by a livery or by any outward signs. I long to see Christian people become more distinct from the world than ever because I am persuaded that, until they are so, the church will never become such a power for blessing people as her Lord intended her to be. It is for the world's good that there should be no alliance between the church and the world by way of compromise ...

The church of God is 'a garden enclosed'. What for, then? Why, that nobody may come into that garden to eat its fruit, but the Lord himself ... If we do not live for the Lord, we are dead while we live. If we do not bring glory to his name, we cannot justify our existence. If we are not as a garden enclosed for Jesus, we are mere bits of wasteland. If we are not fountains sealed for Jesus, we are mere brooks in the valley, which will soon run dry ... Brothers and sisters, your life is to be a stream that flows for the refreshment of him who poured out his life for you! You are to let him drink of the deep fountains of your heart, and no one else may rival Jesus there. You are a spring shut up, a fountain sealed for Jesus, for Jesus only, and that altogether, and always ... This garden is strictly private. Trespassers beware! Should the world, the flesh, or the devil leap over the wall, and stoop down to drink of the crystal fountain of your being, you are to chase them away, lest their leprous lips should defile this spring. All for Jesus: body for Jesus, mind for Jesus, spirit for

Jesus, eyes for Jesus, mouth for Jesus, hands for Jesus, feet for Jesus, all for Jesus.

- Think about the way you use your body, mind, spirit, eyes, mouth, hands, and feet? Are they 'all for Jesus'?

49.

Honorius of Autun in the Song of Songs 4:12-15

A garden locked is my sister, my bride,
a spring locked, a fountain sealed.
Your shoots are an orchard of pomegranates
with all choicest fruits, henna with nard,
nard and saffron, calamus and cinnamon,
with all trees of frankincense, myrrh and aloes,
with all choice spices—
a garden fountain, a well of living water,
and flowing streams from Lebanon.

Honorius of Autun likens the flowers in the garden to different
kinds of Christians. He makes a common medieval distinction
between the contemplative life (dedicated to prayer) and the
active life (dedicated to service). He sees the garden itself as
the church, which is the Garden of Eden restored. The spring
in the garden is Christ nurturing His people through the
Scriptures. But the church is also a spring because what we
receive from Christ is meant to overflow to others. Honorius
(c. 1080-c. 1140) was a popular medieval theologian whose
works were widely read by lay people. Little is known about his
life other than that he was a monk who spent time in England
and Bavaria.

In this garden are a variety of flowers, which represent the
different orders of the elect: martyrs, like roses; confessors, like
violets; virgins, like lilies; and other believers, like other flowers.
The gardener in this garden is Christ. He is also the Bridegroom,
who when he plants by grace also irrigates by teaching. This

'garden' is 'closed' for the benefit of contemplatives – which means fortified against the attack of demons by an angelic guard. It is also 'closed' for the benefit of those who lead the active life, for it is walled about by the defence that its teachers provide against heretics. In this garden the herbs and flowers are the individual believers, blooming with faith and good works.

The comparison here is with the garden of Paradise, which is said to be closed off on every side by a wall of fire and protected by angelic guards (cf. Gen. 3:24), in order that the fire may keep human beings out of it, and the angels may keep the demons away. Thus the Church is the garden of God, surrounded by God's assistance and a fiery wall, and defended by an angelic guard, so that neither demons nor evil humans may be strong enough to harm her. This is said in order that, given the many protectors that safeguard her, their attack may not be feared in the spiritual combat.

In this garden there is a 'spring', to wit, Holy Scripture, by whose stream the Church is watered ... In this garden there is also the 'spring' of baptism, in which the wounds of sins are washed ... The spring washes away our filth, quenches our thirst, restores the image [of God in us].

This spring is Christ, who is the spring of life, from whom there flow streams of 'living water' (John 4:10, 14), that is to say, the gifts of the Holy Spirit, with which he waters the garden of the Church, so that it may bring forth the breaths of life that are flowers. He washes away the filthy deeds of sinners, he quenches the thirst of those who 'thirst for righteousness' (cf. Matt. 5:6) with the fulness of the vision of himself, and he restores to souls the image of God they have lost. He was sealed up in that he was veiled with flesh as with a stamp. Now he is sealed up in that he is concealed from us by the glory of the Father....

But the Church herself is also a 'spring', for she overflows with grace and wisdom, from which there flow streams full of teaching with which she waters the plants in her garden so that they may produce an abundance of outsendings [shoots]. Of these he adds: 'Your outsendings are a paradise of pomegranate trees, with the produce of apple trees.' The garden of the church, watered from the 'spring' of Scripture, puts forth so many shoots that from them a paradise grows up.

- Jesus said: 'If anyone thirsts, let him come to me and drink' (John 7:37).

50.

St John of the Cross on the Song of Songs 4:16

Awake, O north wind,
and come, O south wind!
Blow upon my garden,
let its spices flow.
Let my beloved come to his garden,
and eat its choicest fruits.

St John of the Cross interprets the 'wind' as the Holy Spirit ('wind' and 'Spirit' are the same words in Hebrew). The Spirit dispels spiritual dryness by communicating God's love to us (John 7:37-39). Many medieval and Puritan commentators thought that the warm south wind represents an experience of Christ's love, while the cold north wind represents the hardships that God uses to refine His people. St John of the Cross (1542-1591) was a Spanish monk and mystic who collaborated in monastic and spiritual reform with Teresa of Avila (see #3).

Spiritual dryness hinders the fruition of inner sweetness. Afraid of this dryness, the soul in this verse takes two courses of actions. The first is to shut the door against it through unceasing prayer and devotion. The second is to invoke the Holy Spirit. It is the Spirit who drives away dryness from the soul, and maintains and increases its love for the Bridegroom. The Spirit does this to establish in the soul the exercise of virtue. And all this is done so that the Son of God, the Bridegroom of the soul, may rejoice and delight in the soul more and more, for the soul's only aim is to please the Beloved.

The south wind is a gentle wind that brings rain. It makes the grass and plants grow, it causes flowers to blossom, and it spreads their fragrance abroad. In short, it is the very opposite in its effects of the north wind. It represents the Holy Spirit, who awakens love. For when this divine Breath breathes on the soul, it inflames and refreshes it, it gives life to the will, and stirs up the desires, which were previously at a low ebb and which, when it come to the love of God, were asleep. So we might well say that the Spirit awakens the love between Bridegroom and the soul. So the prayer of the soul to the Holy Spirit is this: 'Blow through my garden.' This garden is the soul itself. For as the soul had previously described itself as a flourishing vineyard because the flowers of virtue in it produce the wine of sweetness, so here it describes itself as a garden because the flowers of perfections and virtues are planted in it and begin to flourish and grow.

With the Holy Spirit breathing through the garden – for this is why the Spirit visits the soul – the Bridegroom, the Son of God, communicates himself to the soul in a profound and loving way. It is for this communion that the Son sends the Holy Spirit ahead of him – as he sent the Apostles – to make ready the home of the soul, his bride. He sends the Spirit to comfort the soul, set its garden in order, open its flowers, reveal its gifts, and adorn it with the tapestry of graces ...

It is good then for every soul to pray that the Holy Spirit would blow through its garden, so that the divine fragrance of God may flow. And since this is so necessary for the happiness of the soul, the bride desires it, and prays for it, in the words of the Song: 'Arise, O north wind, and come, O south wind! Blow upon my garden, and its spices flow.' The soul prays for this, not because of the resulting delight it enjoys, but because of the delight this brings to the Beloved, and because it prepares the way for, and announces the presence of, the Son of God, who comes to rejoice in it.

- 'God's love has been poured into our hearts through the Holy Spirit who has been given to us' (Rom. 5:5).

51.

Richard Sibbes on the Song of Songs 5:1

I came to my garden, my sister, my bride,
I gathered my myrrh with my spice,
I ate my honeycomb with my honey,
I drank my wine with my milk.

Richard Sibbes (see #2) outlines the different ways Christ has been present among His people. (1) In the Old Testament He was present through signs and symbols. (2) During His life on earth He was present in the flesh. (3) When He returns He will be present in glory. (4) In the meantime He is spiritually present through the Holy Spirit. Through the Holy Spirit Christ communicates His presence, through His Word and sacraments. Just as we can experience the sun without bringing it down to earth, so through the Spirit we can experience Christ without bringing Him physically down to earth. We experience Christ as He fuels our love, renews our strength, and comforts our hearts.

Christ promises his gracious presence to his children in response to their desire of it. From the beginning of the world, the church has always had the presence of Christ; for either he has been present in sacrifices, or in other signs of his presence (like the bush, the ark, the pillars of cloud and fire, the temple). Then, secondly, he was more graciously present in his incarnation. And then there is a third and more glorious presence of Christ that all of us wait for, on account of which we are described to be those who wait for the coming of the Lord (1 Thess. 1:10). For the soul of a Christian is never satisfied until it enjoys the highest desire of Christ's presence, which we know well enough must follow in time.

In the meantime, she desires this spiritual presence in a larger and fuller measure, which she in some measure has already had. So, then, Christ is graciously present in his church by his Holy Spirit (Matt. 28:20). It is his promise. When I am gone myself, 'I will not leave you as orphans' (John 14:18), but will leave with you my vicar-general, the Holy Spirit, the Comforter, who shall always be with you.

But how shall we know that Christ is present in us? To know this, we shall not need to pull him from heaven. We may know it in the word and sacraments, and in the communion of saints. These are the conveyances through which he manifests himself, together with the work of his own gracious Spirit in us. We need not take the sun from heaven to know whether or not it be up, or whether it be day. In spring we need not look to the heavens to see whether the sun be near us or not, for looking on the earth we can see green, fresh, lively, strong and vigorous growth. So it is with the presence of Christ. We may know he is present by that light which is in the soul, convincing us of better courses to be taken, of a spiritual life, to know heavenly things, and the difference between them and earthly things, and to set a price upon them. We may know Christ is present when there is, together with light, a heat above nature, the affections are kindled to love the best things, and to find joy in them. We may know Christ is present when, together with heat, there is strength and vigour to enable us to do spiritual duties, framing us to a holy communion with God and one with another. Likewise, we may know Christ is present when there is a cheerfulness and enlargement of spirit, as it is with creatures when the sun approaches. For this reason the church desires Christ, that she may have more light, life, heat, vigour, strength, and that she may be more cheerful and fruitful in duties. The soul, when it is has been made spiritual, still desires a deeper and deeper sense of the presence of Christ to be made better and better.

What a comfort this is to Christians, that they have the presence of Christ so far as shall make them happy, and as much as the earth will allow. Nothing other than heaven itself, or rather Christ in heaven itself, will bring contentment the child of God. In the meantime, his presence in the congregation makes their souls, as it were, heaven.

- Next time you are listening to a sermon or sharing the Lord's Supper, remind yourself that Christ is communicating His presence through the Holy Spirit.

52.

Samuel Rutherford on the Song of Songs 5:1

Eat, friends, drink,
and be drunk with love!

In the writings of Samuel Rutherford (see #11) you can sense his pain that people who are so much in need should reject Christ, when Christ has so much to offer. Rutherford longs to be able to communicate better the boundless beauty and love of Christ. In the meantime 'Adam's fools' waste their love on worthless things. But Rutherford sees the same tendency in his own 'miscarrying heart'. So he ends by calling on Christ to come and satisfy his longings.

O if I could invite and persuade thousands, and ten thousand times ten thousand of Adam's sons, to flock about my Lord Jesus, and to come and take their fill of love! O pity for evermore, that there should be such a one as Christ Jesus, so boundless, so bottomless, and so incomparable in infinite excellency and sweetness, and so few to take him! Oh, oh, you poor, dry, and dead souls, why will you not come hither with your empty vessels, and your barren souls, to this huge, and fair, and deep, and sweet well of life, and fill all your empty vessels? O that Christ should be so large in sweetness and worth, and we so narrow, so pinched, so ebb, and so void of all happiness. And yet people will not take him! They lose their love miserably, who will not bestow it upon this lovely One.

Alas, for thousands of years, Adam's fools, his wasteful heirs, have been wasting and lavishing out their love and their affections upon bits of dead creatures, and broken idols, upon this and that feckless creature; and have not brought their love and their heart to Jesus ...

But let us come near, and fill ourselves with Christ, and let his friends drink, and be drunken, and satisfy our hollow and deep desires with Jesus (Song 5:1). O, come all and drink at this living well; come, drink and live for evermore; come, drink and welcome! 'Welcome,' says our fairest Bridegroom. No one gets Christ with ill will; no man comes and is not welcome. No one comes and rues their voyage; all people speak well of Christ who have been with him. People and angels who know him will say more than I can do, and think more of him than they can say. O, if I were misted and lost in my Lord's love! O, if I were fettered and chained to it! O, sweet pain, to be pained for a sight of him! O living death, O good death, O lovely death, to die for love of Jesus! Oh that I should have a sore heart, and a pained soul, for the want of this and that idol! Woe, woe to the mistakes of my miscarrying heart, that gapes and cries for creatures, and is not pained, and cut, and tortured, and in sorrow, for the want of a soul's-fill of the love of Christ!

O that you would come near, my Beloved! O my fairest One, why do you stand at a distance! Come here, that I may be satiated with your excellent love. Oh for a union! Oh for a fellowship with Jesus! O that I could buy with a price that lovely One, even supposing hell's torments for a while were the price! I cannot believe but Christ will rue upon his pained lovers, and come and ease sick hearts, who sigh and swoon for want of Christ.

- Pray for people dear to you who do not yet see the beauty of Christ.

53.

Richard Sibbes on the Song of Songs 5:2

I slept, but my heart was awake.
A sound! My beloved is knocking.
"Open to me, my sister, my love,
my dove, my perfect one,
for my head is wet with dew,
my locks with the drops of the night."

We sometimes talk of wanting to experience more of Christ. But Richard Sibbes (see #2) says that Christ also wants to experience more of us. And so Christ comes knocking! Full communion with Christ awaits, but we can enjoy communion with Christ in His Word and sacrament.

Christ has never enough of his church till he has it in heaven, which is where the true kisses of the spouse and of Christ will be.

In the meantime, he says, 'Open to me.' Christ had the heart of the spouse in some measure already, but there were yet some corners of the heart that were not as filled with Christ as they should be. He was not so much in her understanding, will, joy, delight, and love as he would be. 'Therefore, open your understanding more and more to embrace me, and divine truths that are offered you. Open your love to comfort me more and more.' Since God in Christ, having condescended to the terms of friendship, to intimate terms of friendship in marriage with us, so the church in her right temper never has enough of Christ, but desires further union and communion ...

Christ also desires them. Indeed, it is his desire for them that breeds their desire for him. 'Open to me, my sister, my love, my dove.' Again his love and pity move him to desire further to come into us. Christ knows what is in our hearts. If he is not there it is because of other things that should not be there. What is in the brain where Christ is absent? A load of worldly projects that are worth nothing. What is our joy if Christ is not there? Worldly joy which cleaves to things worse than itself. If a person were anatomised, and seen into, they would be ashamed of themselves. Christ therefore, out of pity on our souls, would not have the devil there. Christ knows it is good for our souls to give way to him, and therefore he uses all sweet allurements, 'Open to me, my sister, my love.' Christ has never his fill, till he close with the soul perfectly, so that nothing be in the soul above him, nothing equal to him. Therefore 'Open, open.'

Again, Christ sets down to move the church the more to open to him the inconveniences he endured, 'My head is wet with dew, my locks with the drops of the night.' Here he shows what he suffered ... What patience had he in enduring the obstinate spirits of men when he was here on earth! How many indignities he bore from his disciples! And towards the end of his life, his head was not only filled with the drops, but drops of blood came out from him, because of the anguish of his spirit, and the sense of God's wrath for our sins. Upon the cross, what did he endure there! That sense of God's anger there, was only for our sins. 'My God, my God, why have you forsaken me?' (Matt. 27:46).

We therefore labour everyday more and more to have larger and larger affections to Christ. For the soul that loves Christ, the nearer to Christ it is, the more joyful it is. What happiness will be ours when Christ and our souls embrace, and the soul enjoys the thing it loves. But that is not for here, but in heaven. Therefore, in the meantime, with joy we thankfully frequent the places where Christ is present in the word and sacrament. That we may come to have this affection, let us see what our souls are without him – mere dungeons of darkness and confusion, nothing coming from us that is good. This will breed love for the ordinances. And then we shall relish Christ both in the word and sacrament. For he is food for the hungry soul, and requires nothing from us but good appetites. This will make us desire his love and presence.

- Jesus says: 'Behold, I stand at the door and knock. If anyone hears my voice and opens the door, I will come in to him and eat with him, and he with me' (Rev. 3:20).

54.

Robert Murray M'Cheyne on the Song of Songs 5:2-3

A sound! My beloved is knocking.
"Open to me, my sister, my love,
my dove, my perfect one,
for my head is wet with dew,
my locks with the drops of the night."
I had put off my garment;
how could I put it on?
I had bathed my feet;
how could I soil them?

Robert Murray M'Cheyne (see #22) says Christ not only seeks the lost; he also seeks the found (i.e. Christians) so that he might have deeper communion with us and impart greater joy. (This is the mirror of the point Bernard of Clairvaux makes in #32.) M'Cheyne then describes how God seeks us through our daily Bible reading and prayer, and through the preaching and sacraments of the church. These are 'the trysting-place[s]' – the rendezvous of love – where we meet Christ. But sometimes we do not reciprocate the earnestness of Christ, and so these things become dry routines for us.

Christ is seeking believers. It is true that Christ is seeking unconverted souls – he is the Shepherd that seeks the lost sheep. But it is as true that he seeks his own people also, that he may make his abode with them, that their joy may be full. Christ is not done with a soul when he has brought it to forgiveness of sins. It is only then that he begins his regular visits to the soul. In the daily reading of the word, Christ pays daily visits to sanctify the believing soul. In daily prayer, Christ reveals himself to his own in that other way than he does to the world. In the house of God Christ comes to his own and says: 'Peace be with you!' (John 20:19) And in the sacrament he makes himself known in the breaking of bread, so they cry out: 'It is the Lord!' These are all trysting times when the Saviour comes to visit his own. Christ speaks, 'Open to me, my sister, my love, my dove, my perfect one.' O what a meeting of tender words is here, and all applied to a poor sinner who has believed in Christ ...

Observe, too, that Christ waits: 'My head is wet with dew, my locks with the drops of the night.' Christ's patience with unconverted souls is very wonderful. But his patience with his own is still more wonderful. They know how precious he is, and yet they will not let him in. Their sin is all the greater, and yet he waits to be gracious.

Believers are often lazy at these trysting times, and put the Saviour away with many vain excuses.

The hour of daily devotion is a trysting hour with Christ, in which he seeks, and knocks, and speaks, and waits. And yet, dear believers, how often you are lazy and make vain excuses! You have something else to attend to, or you are set upon some worldly comfort, and you do not let the Saviour in.

The Lord's table is the most famous trysting-place with Christ. Yet how often is this opportunity lost through want of attention; through thoughts about worldly things; through an unwillingness to take trouble about it!

'I had put off my garment; how could I put it on? I had bathed my feet; how could I soil them?' Doubtless there are some children of God who did not find Christ last Sabbath-day at the communion table, who went away without refreshment and comfort. See here the cause: it was your own laziness. Christ was knocking, but you would not let him in ... Search your own heart, and you will find the true cause. Perhaps you came without deliberation, without self-examination and prayer, without duly stirring up faith. Perhaps you were thinking about your worldly gains and losses, and you missed the Saviour. Remember, then, he was knocking, and you would not let him in.

- How might seeing Bible reading, prayer, preaching, and communion as 'trysting-place[s]' with Christ change the way you approach them?

55.

Charles Spurgeon on the Song of Songs 5:2-5

I slept, but my heart was awake.
A sound! My beloved is knocking.
"Open to me, my sister, my love,
my dove, my perfect one,
for my head is wet with dew,
my locks with the drops of the night."
I had put off my garment;
how could I put it on?
I had bathed my feet;
how could I soil them?
My beloved put his hand to the latch,
and my heart was thrilled within me.
I arose to open to my beloved,
and my hands dripped with myrrh,
my fingers with liquid myrrh,
on the handles of the bolt.

Charles Spurgeon (see #7) describes how Christ knocks on the door of our hearts as He seeks greater communion with us. Sometimes He knocks through the promises of His Word; sometimes through the afflictions of our lives. He is coming to enjoy the relationship He won through His suffering and death. But Spurgeon then paraphrases the response of the bride to highlight the poor excuses we are prone to make when Christ comes knocking.

The healthiest state for a Christian is that of unbroken and intimate fellowship with the Lord Jesus Christ. 'Abide in me, and I in you' (John 15:4) is the loving precept of our ever-loving Lord. But, alas, brothers and sisters, as in this world our bodies are subject to many sicknesses, so our souls are often sorely afflicted with sin, sickness, and an evil heart of unbelief in departing from the Lord. Spiritual sickness is very common in the church of God, and the root lies in distance from Jesus, following Christ at a distance, and yielding to a drowsy temperament. Without the sun, the flowers pine; without Jesus, our hearts faint ...

At first, the Beloved one simply *knocked*. His object was to enter into fellowship with his church, to reveal himself to her, to unveil his beauties, to comfort her with his presence ...

When you turn to read his word, every promise is a knock. He says, 'Come and enjoy this promise, for it is yes and amen in me' ... In outward providences, every blessing we receive through our Mediator's intercession is a gentle knock from his pierced hand, saying, 'Take this mercy, it comes to you through me; but open to me!' Every affliction is a knock at our door: that wasting sickness, that broken bone, that rebellious child – all these are Christ's knocks, saying, 'These worldly things cannot bring you true rest; open to me! These idols I am breaking, these joys I am removing; open to me, and find in me a comfort for your woes' ... The Lord Jesus Christ has a sweet way of making the word come home to the conscience. Some of you who are the Lord's people, have heard soft and sweet whispers in your heart, saying, 'You are saved; now, my beloved, live in the light of your salvation' ...

Did you notice that powerful argument with which the heavenly lover closed his cry? He said, 'My head is wet with dew, my locks with the drops of the night.' Ah, those drops were not the ordinary dew that fall on the houseless traveller's unprotected head; his head was wet with scarlet dew when 'his sweat became like great drops of blood falling down to the ground' (Luke 22:44). My heart, how vile you are, for you shut out the Crucified! Behold the Man, thorn-crowned and scourged, with traces of the soldiers' spit. Can you close the door on him? Will you despise the One who is 'despised and rejected by men'? Will you grieve the 'man of sorrows', 'acquainted with grief'? (Isa. 53:3) Are you forgetting that he suffered all this for you, for you, when you deserve nothing at his hands? ...

Shall I paraphrase the excuse she made? It is this: 'O Lord, I know that if I am to enter into much fellowship with you, I must pray very differently from what I have done of late, but it is too much trouble. I cannot stir myself to so much energy. My time is so taken up with my business, I am so constantly engaged that I could not afford even a quarter of an hour for retirement. I have to cut my prayers short.' Is this not a miserable excuse? Shall I go on? Shall I tell more of this dishonourable apology? ...

Still, as a wonder of wonders, although shamefully and cruelly treated, the beloved Husband did not go away. We are told that he 'put his hand to the latch', and then the heart of his spouse was moved for him.

- Do you ever respond to the knock of Christ by saying 'it is too much trouble' or 'my time is taken up with my business'?

56.

Richard Sibbes on the Song of Songs 5:6

I opened to my beloved,
but my beloved had turned and gone.
My soul failed me when he spoke.
I sought him, but found him not;
I called him, but he gave no answer.

Richard Sibbes (see #2) says sometimes Christ's presence is felt and sometimes not. The point Sibbes is making is that, even when we do not feel His presence, Christ is at work in our lives. He uses His apparent absence to heighten our longing for Him. During times of spiritual dryness Christ is teaching us to depend on Him, leading us to put sin to death, or purging our pride.

There is a double presence of Christ: felt and not felt

First, the presence felt is when Christ is graciously present and is pleased to let us know as much. This is a heaven upon earth. Souls are in paradise when they feel 'God's love has been poured into our hearts' (Rom. 5:5), and the favourable countenance of God shining upon them. Then they despise the world, the devil, and all, and walks as if they were half in heaven already ...

But, second, there is a presence of Christ that is secret; when he seems to draw us one way, and to drive us another, so that we are both driven and drawn at once; when he seems to put us away, and yet at the same time draws us ... When Christ wrestled with Jacob, though he contended with him, yet at the same time he gave Jacob power to overcome him, to be 'Israel', the one who prevailed over God (Gen. 32:28) ...

It is good to observe this kind of Christ's dealing, so we are not discouraged when we find him absent. If ... we find the Spirit of God moving us to love the word and ordinances, to call upon him by prayer, we may gather there is a hidden, secret presence here that draws us to these things. Indeed, the end of this seeming forsaking and strangeness is to draw us nearer and nearer, and eventually to draw us into heaven to himself. God's people are gainers by all their losses, stronger by all their weaknesses, and the better for all their crosses, whatever they are ...

We should labour, therefore, to answer Christ's dealings with suitable apprehensions of soul when he seems to withdraw some comforts and former experience of his love. It should teach us to depend upon him, and to believe, though we feel no comfort, yes, against comfort, when we feel signs of displeasure. If he can love and support me, and strengthen my soul, and show it a presence of which is suited to me, certainly I should answer thus with my faith, and depend on him ... Therefore I ought in these desertions to cleave to him in life and in death ... Then, God, by a secret work of his Spirit, though he seem to be an enemy, yet he draws his children nearer and nearer to him by such his dealing. All this strangeness is but to mortify some former lust, or consume some former dregs of security ... Labour for an absolute dependence on Christ, with a poverty of spirit in ourselves. This is the goal of Christ's withdrawing of himself, to purge us of self-confidence and pride.

- Christ is present when He seems absent, and He is at work when He seems not to be doing anything.

57.

Charles Spurgeon on the Song of Songs 5:6-8

I sought him, but found him not;
I called him, but he gave no answer.
The watchmen found me
as they went about in the city;
they beat me, they bruised me,
they took away my veil,
those watchmen of the walls.
I adjure you, O daughters of Jerusalem,
if you find my beloved,
that you tell him
I am sick with love.

Like James Durham (see #33), Charles Spurgeon (see #7) sees the watchmen as church ministers. But here Spurgeon thinks they are too harsh. They rightly brought conviction of sin, but, instead of then applying the comfort of the gospel, they made her wound worse. Spurgeon goes on to describe how our spiritual lives grow weak when we are not enjoying communion with Christ. But such 'love-sickness' is a blessing when it drives us back to Christ. God increases our longing so that He might satisfy us all the more.

'I sought him,' said she, 'but found him not.' 'I went to the house of God; the sermon was sweet, but it was not sweet to me, for *he* was not there. I went to the communion table, and the ordinance was a feast of fat things to others, but not to me, for *he* was not there ...'

She went to his ministers. Perhaps they had never passed through her experience; perhaps they were mere hirelings. However it might be, they smote her. Sometimes the truthful preaching of the gospel will smite a child of God when they get out of their walk with God, and it is right it should be so. But they did more than smite; they 'bruised' her until she began to bleed from the wounds given by the very men whom she hoped would have comforted her. Oh, cruel work to pull off her veil and expose her, when she was already wretched enough! Sometimes a sharp sentence from a true minister may set a poor soul in the stocks who ought rather to have been comforted ...

The heart is panting to be brought once more under the apple tree (Song 2:3). She has known in days past what it is to be brought into his banqueting house, and to see the banner of love waved over her (Song 2:4). And she therefore cries to have love visits renewed. It is a panting after communion.

Gracious hours, my dear friends, are never perfectly at ease except they are in a state of nearness to Christ. For mark you, when they are not near to Christ, they lose their peace. The nearer to Jesus, the nearer to the perfect calm of heaven. There is no peace for the person who does not dwell constantly under the shadow of the cross. For Jesus is our peace, and if he is absent, our peace is absent too. The Christians without fellowship with Christ lose all their life and energy. They are like a dead thing. Though saved, they lie like a lumpish log. They are without vivacity and without animation till Jesus comes. The heart when near to Jesus has strong pulsations. For since Jesus is in that heart, it is full of life, of vigour, and of strength. Peace, liveliness, vigour – all depend upon the constant enjoyment of communion with Christ Jesus. The soul of a Christian never knows what joy means in its true solidity, except when they sit like Mary at Jesus' feet (Luke 10:39).

Beloved, all the joys of life are nothing to us. We have melted them all down in our crucible, and found them to be dross. You and I have tried earth's vanities, and they cannot satisfy us.

Indeed they do not give a morsel of meat to satisfy our hunger. Being in a state of dissatisfaction with all mortal things, we have learned through divine grace that none except Jesus can make our souls glad ... What bread is to the hungry, clothes to the naked, 'the shade of a great rock in a weary land' (Isa 32:2), such is Jesus Christ to us. Therefore, if we are not conscious of having him, little marvel if our spirit cries in the words of the Song, 'I adjure you, O daughters of Jerusalem, if you find my beloved, that you tell him I am sick with love.' Such is the character of this love-sickness.

Blessed love-sickness! Notice the comforts which belong to this state. It is impossible for Christ to set you longing after him without intending to give himself to you. It is like when a great man makes a feast. He first puts plates on the table, and then afterwards there comes the food. Your longings and desires are the empty plates to hold the food. He makes you long, and so he will certainly satisfy your longings. Remember, again, that he will give you himself *all the sooner for the bitterness of your longings.*

> Love divine, how sweet thou art!
> When shall I find my willing heart
> all taken up by thee?
> I thirst, I faint, I die to prove
> the fullness of redeeming love,
> the love of Christ to me! (Charles Wesley)

- 'It is impossible for Christ to set you longing after Him without intending to give Himself to you.'

58.

Richard Sibbes on the Song of Songs 5:8-9

She: *I adjure you, O daughters of Jerusalem,*
if you find my beloved,
that you tell him
I am sick with love.
Others: *What is your beloved more than another beloved,*
O most beautiful among women?
What is your beloved more than another beloved,
that you thus adjure us?

Richard Sibbes (see #2) commends what he calls 'holy conference' or 'gospel conversations'. The bride shares her need and the daughters of Jerusalem respond by asking her about Christ. One thing leads to another and, as a result, she feels her love for Christ rekindled.

We see here the excellent use of *holy conference*. The church coming to the daughters of Jerusalem, speaking of Christ her beloved, says that she is 'sick with love' (Song 5:8), and the daughters of Jerusalem are inquisitive to know Christ more and more. Here is the benefit of holy conference and gospel conversations. One thing draws on another, and that draws on another, till at length the soul is warmed and kindled with the consideration and meditation of heavenly things. That which is little in the beginning may lead on to great matters. This question to the church breeds questions in others ('What is your beloved?') From this, upon the description of her beloved, her heart is kindled, and she finds her beloved. So talking of holy and heavenly things is good for others and ourselves also.

It is good for others, as it was good for the daughters of Jerusalem here. For they are stirred up to be inquisitive about Christ. And it was good for the church herself, for she took the opportunity to make a large commendation of Christ, through which she found much comfort ...

This may remind us to spend our time fruitfully in good conversations when appropriate. We know not, when we begin, where we may end up. Our souls may be carried up to heaven before we are aware, for the Spirit will enlarge our conversation and move it from one thing to another.

- Ask a Christian how God is speaking to them through His Word or how they have been enjoying Christ's love.

59.

John of Ford on the Song of Songs 5:10

My beloved is radiant and ruddy,
distinguished among ten thousand.

John of Ford develops the idea of Christ being 'radiant'. Christ is the Light whose light lights up the stars. But humanity rejected the Light and plunged itself into darkness. So the Light took on flesh to come among us and dispel our darkness. More than that, He has shone His light *within* us, both to transform our inner darkness, and to cover us with this righteousness. John of Ford (c. 1140-1214) was the abbot of a Cistercian monastery in Forde in Dorset, England. His sermons on the Song of Songs were an attempt to complete the series begun by Bernard of Clairvaux (see #5).

When you ask what my 'Beloved from the Beloved' is like, I [the Bride is speaking] have an answer right on the tip of my tongue: just as the Father is supremely beautiful and supremely desirable, so too, in every respect, is his Only-Begotten, 'shining bright' from the 'shining bright', 'ruddy' from the 'ruddy' ...

So then, O light most beautiful, O radiance of light eternal, this is what you were from the very beginning, this is what you were, O ancient loveliness, in your ancient days, in the years of your eternity. This is what you were, O Lord Jesus - wise, true, holy, benevolent but this you were at once for yourself and for your Father ... You were the fullness of joy for him, as he was for you.

Since, however, you were not only Light's Light but also the fountainhead of light, you suddenly shone in those that you decree to be sharers in so great a good – and this in order that this same good might be manifested to your creation and shared by it. You summoned the stars, and they said, 'Here we are.' And for you they delighted to give light, eternally rejoicing in you, their incommunicable good, and shimmering perpetually and passionately in the presence of you, their Source.

Where we are concerned, however, whom you created to delight in you, but who withdrew from you and wanted to keep our strength for ourselves – we walked head-long into the darkness of ignorance and weakness. This was a deep darkness indeed, so deep that we had no ... awareness that we were fallen or that we were continuing to go head over heels downward. Even then, O true Light, you were shining in the midst of this darkness of ours; but our darkness did not comprehend you (cf. John 1:5). You who are never absent were near us, but we were far from you; we were exiled in a realm far from your light, in a realm of darkness, in the realm of 'the shadow of death' (Ps. 23:4) ...

Therefore, you – the dawning splendour of eternal Light – ... became not only a lamp that our eyes could see but also one that our hands could touch ... You burst forth from the bright womb of the Virgin, O brightest of lights, and there you really did set 'your tabernacle in the sun' (Ps. 19:4) ... You broke up the night of our ignorance by flashing forth in the darkness, and you showed the works of darkness up; for out of the cloud of your flesh, you thundered the threat of judgment and the news of the kingdom. You shimmered with signs and wonders, and you showed that you are our true and unique salvation by taking away our sins.

Nevertheless, it would have been fruitless for you to show us these things on the outside unless you also shone within us. So because you were also Holiness, you count it a matter of first importance to accord us your mercy by setting fear of you within us, and in this way you make us holy, turning us away from our own darkness and mercifully drawing us to you, the true Light.

Finally, because you were also benevolence, and in order that you might attire in splendour those who had garbed themselves in faith's confession, and thus we might 'walk becomingly as in the day' (Rom. 13:13 ASV), you covered us with the light of your righteousness. You conferred benevolence on us by infusing the Spirit of your grace, and 'our earth brought forth its fruit' (Ps. 85:12 WYC).

- The sons of ignorance and night
  may dwell in the eternal Light,
  through the eternal Love. (Thomas Binney, 1826)

60.

Richard Sibbes on the Song of Songs 5:10-16

My beloved is radiant and ruddy,
distinguished among ten thousand.
His head is the finest gold;
his locks are wavy, black as a raven ...
His mouth is most sweet,
and he is altogether desirable.
This is my beloved and this is my friend,
O daughters of Jerusalem.

Richard Sibbes (see #2) cautions against making too much of the details in the bride's description of her beloved. The central point is that Christ is altogether lovely. And, therefore, He is the one who is worthy of all our love and affection.

In speaking of these particulars we have to be very wary, for we have no foundation to interpret them beyond their general truth. Without doubt the Spirit of God here intended to set out the large affection that the church had for Christ, rather than to insinuate any great particularity in every one of these descriptions. Therefore let us only take those things that are of ease to explain: ... Christ is altogether lovely.

And if Christ be so lovely, then on him alone should we place the best of our affections. Is it not a pity that we lose so much of our affections as we do upon other things? Christ is altogether lovely. So why should we dote on other things so much, and set up idols in our hearts above Christ? Is he altogether lovely, and shall he not have altogether our lovely affections, especially when we are commanded, under pain of a curse, to love the Lord Jesus? Anathema to those that love not Christ (1 Cor. 16:22). Let us therefore labour to place all our sweet affections – our love, joy, and delight – upon this object, this lovely deserving object, Christ, who is 'altogether lovely'. Like letting a pure stream, as it were, run through a dirty channel, so are our affections if we let them run after the things of the world, which are worse than ourselves. In this way, we lose our affections and ourselves. Therefore let the whole stream of our affections be carried to Christ.

Love Christ, and whatever is his, for he being altogether lovely, all that comes from him is lovely. His promises, his directions, his counsels, his children, his sacraments, are all lovely. Whatever has the stamp of Christ upon it, let us love it. We cannot bestow our hearts better than to lose ourselves in the love of Christ, and to forget ourselves and the love of anything else. Yes, to hate all in comparison with him, and to account all 'loss' and 'rubbish' compared with Christ (Phil. 3:8), is the only way to find ourselves. And indeed we have a better condition in him than in the world or in ourselves. Severed from him, our condition is vain, and will come to nothing. But the condition we have in him is admirable and everlasting. We cannot conceive the happiness to which we poor wretches will be advanced in Christ, and what excellent things remain for us, which come from the love of God to us in Christ, who is so altogether lovely. Therefore let us labour to kindle in our hearts an affection towards Christ as much as we can, considering that he is thus lovely.

- Lord it is my chief complaint,
  that my love is weak and faint;
  yet I love thee and adore,
  oh, for grace to love thee more! (William Cowper, 1768)

61.

Anne Dutton on the Song of Songs 5:10

My beloved is radiant and ruddy,
distinguished among ten thousand.

Anne Dutton takes the 'ruddy' appearance of Christ to be a picture of His atoning blood. One reason Christ is beautiful to His bride is that He bore the punishment of her sin in her place. Dutton (1692-1765) was a Reformed Baptist theologian who corresponded with the leaders of the evangelical awakening such as George Whitefield. She published around fifty books, some under a pseudonym and others as extended letters.

Christ was 'ruddy' with respect to the imputation of sin. Sin is a red or bloody colour, since it speaks of death to the soul, wherever it is found. And therefore, when the Lord sets forth the sins of his people in their aggravated guilt and the punishment they deserve, he compares them to scarlet and crimson (Isa. 1:18) ...

The elect of God in their fallen state were red with sin, red through the declaration of divine vengeance in the curse of the law. And we would have been forever red under the fierce wrath of God, and his fiery indignation, had God not been in Christ reconciling them to himself, not imputing to them their trespasses (2 Cor. 5:19). And God in order not to impute sin to his people instead imputed all their sins to his dear Son (Isa. 53:6).

God the Father in infinite grace to us took all the iniquities of his chosen, and bundled them up, as it were, into one iniquity, one huge mass of sin, which he laid upon his own Son. As, in the type, all the iniquities and transgressions of God's people Israel were laid on the head of the scapegoat on the Day of Atonement, so were all the sins of all those who shall be saved laid, or made to meet, on Christ on that great atoning Day when our Great High Priest offered up himself, that one great sacrifice, once for all, to satisfy divine justice, and make peace between God and us, to make God and his people for ever at one. And this laying of sin on Christ was by imputation (2 Cor. 5:21). He has made him to be sin for us who knew no sin, that we might be made the righteousness of God in him.

God the Father made Christ sin for us, or made him our sin, by transferring, or carrying over, our sin onto him. He put him in our place that we might be put in his place. He made him sin, that we might be made righteousness. It was his human nature alone that was capable of obeying; but since that human nature was personally united to the Son of God, so his obedience was the obedience of the whole Person, and so was rightly called the righteousness of God, with a Divine Glory upon it.

Oh, the transcendent excellence of this glorious robe, which our Lord created to be the justifying righteousness of his people! It has not only the utmost perfections of a creature in it, but the rays of infinite glory also resplendently shining there! Oh, who would choose to dress himself up in a creature-righteousness were it ever so perfect; much less in the filthy rags of a sinner's obedience, to stand in before a God of infinite Glory, when there is such a beautiful garment, such a transcendent, glorious robe provided, to clothe every naked soul that desires to be found in it! The riches of divine grace displayed here will be the eternal admiration of all the saved ones! Oh how beautiful is Christ to the eye of his sinful spouse as *ruddy*, while in condescending grace his *white*, his glorious self, stoops down to be made sin for her!

- Feel the weight of your sin bearing down on you. Then see that burden lifted from your shoulders and borne by Christ at the cross.

62.

Anne Dutton on the Song of Songs 5:10

My beloved is radiant and ruddy,
distinguished among ten thousand.

Anne Dutton (see #61) expands the description of Christ as
'distinguished among ten thousand' by showing how His glory
outshines all other glories: Christ is uniquely beautiful. But
He is also unique in being able to communicate some of His
beauty to His bride: Christ makes us beautiful by enabling us
to share in His beauty.

All the glories, beauties, and excellencies which are dispersed
among the children of men, and shine, as so many scattered
beams, among all their innumerable multitude, meet together in
his sun-like face, and are infinitely out-shone by his incomparable
brightness! As the scattered beams meet in the sun's body, so all
created excellencies meet in Christ, as in their centre, source,
and origin. There they shine with the most bright radiant glory,
and from him they cast their rays upon all the creatures in both
worlds. Do creatures shine like twinkling stars? Christ is the sun
which casts all their starry lustre!

As all created excellencies meet in Christ, so also do uncreated
excellencies! He who is fairer than the children of men, to whom
none in the heavens may be compared, is God by nature, the
LORD, Jehovah! God and man in one Person! And as such, the
church's Beloved. And therefore he must be the chief among
ten thousand! He is so in himself, and he is so in her esteem.
All glories meet in him universally, perfectly, and perpetually.

He is beauty without deformity; light without darkness; joy without sorrow; and life without end! Oh, this precious Jesus! What a ravishing object is he to those souls who have an eye to see his incomparable glory! None but blind souls dote upon creature excellencies – those glow-worm glories sparkling in the night of nature's ignorance. No, those who have an eye of faith to see Jesus have beheld in him such a transcendent brightness that puts out the light of all creature beauties, and makes them appear, when compared with his, to be mere darkness. The saints have seen a super-excelling glory in Christ that attracts their whole soul to him, and makes them say, 'None but Christ! None but Christ!'

As Christ is beauty in himself, so he has it for his spouse. The beauty of other husbands can neither be accounted, nor communicated to a deformed bride. But Christ makes his spouse beautiful in his beauty, her beauty perfect through his beauty, which he puts on her (Ezek. 16:14). He makes her pure in his purity; righteous in his obedience; clean in his blood; white in his victories; acceptable in his acceptability; wise in his wisdom; strong in his strength; and every way glorious in himself. And in this way also, he is to her the chief among ten thousand!

None like Christ, this precious Jesus, to his spouse, in heaven or in earth! He is precious in his person, as the head and husband of the church. And he is precious in his office, as the only Saviour of the body. His personal glories are immense! His riches, unsearchable! His love, boundless! His compassions, deep! His faithfulness, great! His wisdom, infinite! And his power, almighty! And his salvation is full, free, and eternal! And, in a word, he is what *he* is, and what he is in himself. That he is to his Spouse! He is in himself an incomprehensible, eternal fulness of all life and glory! And he is to her, a communicative fountain of all life and glory, through all times, and unto all eternity! And therefore, well might the spouse say, 'My beloved is radiant and ruddy, distinguished among ten thousand!'

- What is captivating you at the moment? Dutton says such things are simply creatures that 'shine like twinkling stars' while 'Christ is the sun which casts all their starry lustre!'

63.

John Owen on the Song of Songs 5:12

*His eyes are like doves
beside streams of water,
bathed in milk,
sitting beside a full pool.*

In his book *Communion with God,* John Owen shows his
readers the beauty and grace of the person of Christ, so he
turns to chapter 5 of the Song of Songs. He expounds each
aspect of the description of the beloved. Here he explores the
significance of the eyes of Christ. John Owen (1616-1683) was
a Puritan minister, and perhaps England's greatest theologian.
He was vice-chancellor of Oxford University during the
Commonwealth, but after the restoration of the monarch he
largely devoted his time to writing.

The next thing described is his *eyes.* 'His eyes are like doves
beside streams of water, bathed in milk, sitting beside a full
pool.' The reason for this allusion is obvious: doves are tender
birds, not birds of prey ... Their being washed in milk – or clear,
white, crystal water – adds to their beauty ... Eyes are for sight,
discernment, knowledge, and acquaintance with the things that
can be seen. So what is intended here is the knowledge, the
understanding, the discerning Spirit of Christ Jesus. Four things
are ascribed to them: (1) tenderness; (2) purity; (3) discerning;
and (4) glory:

1. *The tenderness and compassion of Christ* toward his church is
here intended. He looks on us with the eyes of a gall-less dove,

with tenderness and careful compassion, without anger, fury or thoughts of revenge ...

2. *Purity* – like the eyes of a dove washed pure. This may be taken either for the ... purity of his sight and knowledge in himself, or the delight he takes in seeing purity in others (Hab. 1:13; Ps. 5:4-5). But here lies the excellence of his love to us, that he takes care to take away our filth and stains that he may delight in us. And, seeing we are so defiled, this could be done in no other way than through his own blood (Eph. 5:25-27) ...

3. *Discerning.* He sees like doves – quickly, clearly, thoroughly. He sees to the bottom of whatever he looks on (Rev. 1:14; 2:23; John 2:24-25) ... No humble, broken, contrite soul shall lose one sigh or groan after him, and communion with him. No pant of love or desire is hidden from him – he sees in secret. No glorious performance of the most glorious hypocrite will prevail with him – for his eyes see through everything, and the filth of their hearts lies naked before him.

4. *Beauty and glory* are also intended here ... He is the wisdom of God's eternal wisdom itself; his understanding is infinite. What spots and stains are in our knowledge! When it is made perfect, yet it will still be finite and limited. His is without spot of darkness, and without foil of limitedness. Thus, then, is he beautiful and glorious.

- Think of the eyes of Christ looking on you with tenderness, compassion, purity, and discernment. By faith, return His look and see His beauty and glory.

64.

James Durham on the Song of Songs 5:13

His cheeks are like beds of spices,
mounds of sweet-smelling herbs.
His lips are lilies, dripping liquid myrrh.

James Durham (see #13) says the words of Christ are sweet, as if his lips dripped with 'liquid myrrh'. Christ is not simply communicating information to us. He communicates something of Himself and of His love. As you read the Bible, Christ is telling you personally, through the Spirit, how He thinks about you and what He has done for you. It's a message we need to hear day by day: like a wife being told by her husband that he loves her, so Christ tells you.

This must be an excellent Beloved, she says, who speaks much, and never a word falls from his lips which is not precious and savoury, like a cordial to the souls of his people, especially in their fainting fits. And there is ever some good word to be received from him. Far from the rough speeches that many use, but pleasant and kindly are all his words!

There is a special loveliness in the words of our Lord Jesus to his people. How much this was seen throughout chapter 4 of this Song? And what love appears in all his promises? Indeed, in the titles that he gives his people, every one is big with strong consolation for them. Christ's words have a special refreshing power in them, and can comfort, refresh and sustain drooping sick souls. He sends out his word and it heals them. Those who love Christ truly also have a high esteem for his word, and are delighted with it. And where there is little esteem of his word, there is little esteem of him. Those who have tasted the sweetness of the word highly esteem Christ himself. The word of Christ is as a word from Christ's own lips, and sweetly sets out his thoughts of love to sinners. It is good to read of Christ's loveliness out of his own word, and from his own mouth.

Where there has been a sweetness felt in the word, it should be turned over to the commendation of Christ since he spoke it as proof of the reality of his excellent worth. The word is never rightly used, even though it should fill the head with knowledge, until it be savoury to the inward person and spiritual senses. And it's that which makes it lovely, when the virtue and consolation that flows from it is felt.

All the consolations of the word do not come out at once, neither can we receive them in that way. We receive its comfort in drops, little and little, continually. And therefore daily should we draw from these wells of salvation.

- Think of the last sermon you heard and receive it as a personal message to you from Christ.

65.

John Owen on the Song of Songs 5:16

His mouth is most sweet,
and he is altogether desirable.
This is my beloved and this is my friend,
O daughters of Jerusalem.

In the following excerpt John Owen ends his description of Christ (see #63) by outlining all the different ways that Christ is 'altogether lovely' (KJV). Owen wants us to feel the culminative force of his description. From whichever angle you look at Christ, He is lovely.

The spouse concludes everything in this general assertion: 'he is altogether desirable' – altogether to be desired or beloved. It is as if she should have said: 'I have thus reckoned up some of the perfections of creatures (things of most value, price, usefulness, beauty, glory, here below), and compared some of the excellencies of my Beloved to them ... But all this comes short of his perfections and beauty, for he is altogether desirable.'

- Lovely in his person – in the glorious all-sufficiency of his deity, gracious purity and holiness of his humanity, authority and majesty, love and power.

- Lovely in his birth and incarnation; when he was rich, for our sakes becoming poor – taking the part of flesh and blood, to be like us; being made of a woman that for us he might be made under the law, even for our sakes.

- Lovely in the whole course of his life, and the more than angelical holiness and obedience which, in the depth of poverty and persecution, he exercised there – doing good, receiving evil, blessing others, and being cursed, reviled, reproached, all his days.

- Lovely in his death; indeed, in this he is most lovely to sinners – never more glorious and desirable than when he was broken, dead, on the cross. For then he had carried all our sins into a land of forgetfulness; then he had made peace and reconciliation for us; then he had procured life and immortality for us.

- Lovely in his whole employment, in his great undertaking – in his life, death, resurrection, ascension; being a mediator between God and us, to recover the glory of God's justice, and to save our souls – to bring us to an enjoyment of God, who were set at such an infinite distance from him by sin.

- Lovely in the glory and majesty with which he is crowned. Now he is set down at the right hand of the Majesty on high, where, though he is terrible to his enemies, yet he is full of mercy, love, and compassion, toward his beloved ones.

- Lovely in all those supplies of grace and consolations, in all the dispensations of his Holy Spirit, in which his saints are made partakers.

- Lovely in all the tender care, power, and wisdom, which he exercises in the protection, safe-guarding and delivery of his church, in the midst of all the oppositions and persecutions to which they are exposed.

- Lovely in all his ordinances, and the whole of that spiritually glorious worship which he has appointed to his people, by which they draw near and have communion with him and his Father.

- Lovely and glorious in the vengeance he takes, and will finally execute, on the stubborn enemies of himself and his people.

- Lovely in the pardon he has purchased and dispenses in the reconciliation he has established, in the grace he communicates, in the comforts he administers, in the peace and joy he gives his saints, in his assured preservation of them to glory.

What shall I say? There is no end of his excellencies and desirableness: 'This is my beloved and this is my friend, O daughters of Jerusalem.'

- Take a moment to turn each of John Owen's points into a prayer of praise.

66.

Anne Dutton on the Song of Songs 5:16

His mouth is most sweet,
and he is altogether desirable.
This is my beloved and this is my friend,
O daughters of Jerusalem.

Anne Dutton (see #61) invites us to do a thought experiment.
Think of something you find desirable. Now identify what
makes it so desirable. Then use your imagination to expand
that desire still further. The desire leads to Christ, says Dutton.
All our desires meet in Christ. If angels or glorified saints were
to do the same exercise with all their expanded capacities, they
would still arrive at Christ as the ultimate object of their desire.
Even God the Father has all His desires met in Christ. So our
true happiness will be to gaze forever on the beauty of Christ.

Christ is the sum of all blessedness in himself, so the centre of
her soul, the sum of her delights, yes, of all delights! As she here
expressly says, 'He is all desires!' That is, all things that are truly
desirable meet in him, universally, unchangeably, essentially, and
eternally! And it is as if she should say, 'Stretch your thoughts to
the utmost extent of all that is desirable, in persons or things,
in all worlds, in all times, and unto all eternity, and this my
Beloved is! He is all desires! ...

Yes, let all, even the most enlarged saints on earth and the
more capacious saints in heaven, with all the hosts of angels in
their bright understandings, stretch their thoughts to the utmost
extent, of all they can possibly desire, both particularly and

universally, for present and future, even to an endless eternity, and this my Beloved is! He is all desires! All beauties in their vast variety perpetually meet, and radiantly shine, in all their bright lustre in the one, unchangeable and eternal glory of his great person ...

Such are the infinite perfections of his glorious person that he is God's delight! 'My soul,' says he, 'delights in him' (Isa. 42:1, paraphrase). The soul of God the Father, if I may so say, finds all its desires, satisfactorily filled to an infinity and eternity of delight with the immense, unchangeable and endless glories of his own Son! And therefore the spouse might well glory in this, her Beloved, since he is such a great person, of such boundless and immense glories, that he is the Beloved even of God himself! He is ALL desires! What could she say more?

The glories of Christ are a bottomless ocean that can never be fathomed; a boundless sea that can never be sailed over; an infinite height that can never be reached; and an eternal length that can never be ended! And as, in their full variety and entire beauty, they will always abide the same in his unchangeable Person, so they will always appear new to his spouse, and admit of new displays to all finite minds by reason of their immensity in his infinite Person! Therefore he will satisfy all his saints and angels with the vision of his face to an endless eternity, and so transport them with new delights, under the new and increasing displays of his infinite glory ... And in this way, he will make it impossible for them to lose their bliss by casting an eye from off him ... And the nearer the saints come to perfection, the deeper they dive into, and the more intensely they delight in, the personal glories of Christ.

Thus Ephesians 4:13 says: 'Till we all come in the unity of the faith and of the knowledge of the Son of God, to a perfect man, unto the measure of the stature of the fulness of Christ (KJV).' The happiness of Christ's spouse in the height of perfect glory will consist in the knowledge of her Beloved, in his personal excellencies as the Son of God, or in a perfect discerning of him, and eternal communion with him, in all his immense glories as the Son of God! When to endless ages, to his eternal honour, and to her eternal joy in him and endearment to him, she will say of him, as here in Song of Songs 5:16: 'He is altogether lovely!' or, 'all desires!'

- What is top of your list of desires today? How is that desire truly and ultimately met in Christ?

67.

John Flavel on the Song of Songs 5:16

His mouth is most sweet,
and he is altogether desirable.
This is my beloved and this is my friend,
O daughters of Jerusalem.

The Reformed tradition has often spoken of the threefold office of Christ: He is our Prophet, Priest, and King. John Flavel picks up this idea and shows how Christ is altogether lovely in these offices. In each role Christ perfectly meets some aspect of our need. So knowing Christ as our Prophet, Priest, and King brings unspeakable comfort to needy sinners like us. Flavel (c. 1627-1691) was a Puritan minister in Devon, England. When forced to leave the Church of England at the Great Ejection in 1662, he continued preaching on the edge of the law, until he was finally allowed to start a non-conformist congregation in Dartmouth.

Christ is altogether lovely in his person: deity dwelling in flesh (John 1:14). The wonderful union and perfection of the divine and human natures in Christ render him an object of admiration and adoration to angels and people (1 Tim. 3:16). God never presented to the world such a vision of glory before. And then consider how the human nature of our Lord Jesus Christ is replenished with all the graces of the Spirit (John 3:34). This makes him fairer than the children of men, grace being poured into his lips (Ps. 45:2). If a small measure of grace in the saints make them such sweet and desirable companions, what must the riches and fulness of the Spirit of grace, filling Jesus

Christ without measure, make him in the eyes of believers? O what a glory and lustre must it stamp upon him!

He is also altogether lovely in his offices: for let us but consider the suitableness, fulness, and comfort of them.

First, the suitableness of the offices of Christ to the miseries and wants of people. We are by nature blind and ignorant, at best but groping in the dim light of nature after God (Acts 17:27). But Christ is a light to lighten the Gentiles (Isa. 49:6). When this great prophet came into the world, then did the dayspring from on high visit us (Luke 1:78). The state of nature is a state of alienation from, and enmity against, God. But Christ comes into the world as our Priest and as an atoning sacrifice, making peace by the blood of his cross (Col. 1:20). All the world, by nature, are in bondage and captivity to Satan, a lamentable slavery. But Christ comes with kingly power to rescue sinners, as a prey from the mouth of the terrible one.

Secondly, let the fulness of his offices be also considered by reason of which 'he is able to save to the uttermost those who draw near to God through him' (Heb. 7:25). The three offices, comprising in them all that our souls need, become an universal relief to all our wants.

Therefore, thirdly, the offices of Christ offer unspeakable comfort to the souls of sinners. If light be pleasant to our eyes, how pleasant is that light of life springing from the Sun of righteousness (Mal. 4:2)! If a pardon be sweet to a condemned criminal, how sweet is the sprinkled blood of Jesus to the trembling conscience of a law-condemned sinner? If a rescue from a cruel tyrant be sweet to a poor captive, how sweet it is for enslaved sinners to hear the voice of liberty and deliverance proclaimed by Jesus Christ? Out of the several offices of Christ, as out of so many fountains, all the promises of the new covenant flow, as so many soul-refreshing streams of peace and joy. All the promises of illumination, counsel and direction flow from his *prophetic office*; all the promises of reconciliation, peace, pardon, and acceptance flow from his *priestly office*, with sweet streams of joy, and spiritual comforts; all the promises of converting, increasing, defending, directing, and supplying grace flow from the *kingly office* of Christ. Indeed, all the promises may be reduced to the three offices, and Jesus Christ is altogether lovely in his offices.

- What need weighs heavily on your heart today? How does Christ as our Prophet, Priest, or King meet that need?

68.

Richard Sibbes on the Song of Songs 6:1-2

Others: *Where has your beloved gone,*
O most beautiful among women?
Where has your beloved turned,
that we may seek him with you?
She: *My beloved has gone down to his garden*
to the beds of spices,
to graze in the gardens
and to gather lilies.

If I share a cake with people, then I end up with less cake. But if I share Christ with people, I don't end up with less of Christ. In fact, I may experience more of Christ in the process. That's the point Richard Sibbes (see #2) makes as he speaks of the bride's willingness to point others to her beloved. Sibbes then says Christ is found among the lilies, which Sibbes takes as a picture of Christians. Christians are pure, like lilies, because of the purity Christ has given us. Sibbes links the lilies of the Song of Songs with the lilies in Matthew 6:28-30, which are signs of God's care.

The church is not squeamish, but directly answers the question. For there is no envy in spiritual things. One may have as much as another, and all alike. Envy is not found for those things that are not divisible. In other things, the more one has, another has the less. But there is no envy in grace and glory because all may share alike. Therefore there is no envy in the answer, as if she denied the daughters of Jerusalem the enjoyment of her beloved. No. If you will know, says she, I will tell you directly where my beloved has gone.

'My beloved has gone down to his garden to the beds of spices, to graze in the gardens and to gather lilies' ... The church of God has two gardens or paradises after the first paradise (which was a picture of them): the paradise of the church and the paradise of heaven. Those that are good plants in the paradise of the church will be glorious plants also in the paradise of heaven ...

Christians are compared to lilies for their purity and whiteness, unspotted in justification; and for their endeavours in sanctity and holiness, in which also eventually they shall be wholly unspotted. It is the end for which they were chosen: to 'be holy and blameless before him in love' (Eph. 1:4). God and Christ look upon them without blame, not as they are here defiled and spotted, but as they intend, little by little, to purge and purify themselves by the Spirit that is in them, that they may be altogether without blame.

They are lilies being clothed with the white garment of Christ's righteousness. Not having a natural whiteness and purity, the whiteness and purity of God's children is borrowed. All their beauty and garments are taken from another's wardrobe. The church is all glorious within, but she borrows her glory as the moon borrows her light from the sun. The church's excellence is borrowed. It is her own, but it is hers by gift. But now that it is hers, it is hers forever ...

So God's children have an excellence and glory in them which, though it is not from them, yet it is theirs by gift, and eternally theirs. Therefore let them comfort themselves against all the censures of sinful people that labour to trample them under foot, and think basely and meanly of them, as the cast-offs of the world. Let the unworthy world think of them as they will, they are lilies in God's esteem ... And whatever our wants, God will take care of his own. Christ uses this argument when he says that, just as God clothes the lilies of the field with an excellent beauty, how much more will he take care of you,

O you of little faith? (Matt. 6:29). Does he care for lilies which are here today and tomorrow are cast into the oven? And shall he not care for the lilies of paradise, the living lilies, those holy reasoning lilies? Undoubtedly he will.

- Look closely at a flower and reflect on its beauty. Then meditate on Matthew 6:28-33.

69.

Gregory of Nyssa on the Song of Songs 6:3

I am my beloved's and my beloved is mine;
he grazes among the lilies.

Gregory of Nyssa (see #8) describes these words in Song of
Songs as the 'definition of perfection' because it describes
someone who is no longer living for anything other than
Christ. We become like a picture of Christ. This is actually
the way we were meant to be, in our 'primordial blessedness',
when we were first made in the image of God. So we become
more ourselves, rather than *less* ourselves, as we become like
Christ. We become a reflection of Christ as we gaze upon His
image. Our hopes and fears are shaped by our commitment to
Christ, and not by selfish gain.

The next line, which the pure and spotless Bride speaks when
she says, *'I am for my kinsman, and my kinsman is for me,'* is the norm
and definition of perfection in virtue. For through these words
we learn that the purified soul is to have nothing within her
save God and is to look upon nothing else. Rather must she so
cleanse herself of every material concern and thought that she
is entirely, in her whole being, transposed into the intelligible
and immaterial realm and makes of herself a supremely vivid
image of the prototypical Beauty.

Thus the person who sees on the flat surface of a board
a sketch that closely approximates the form of a particular
prototype declares that the form of both is the same: he will
say both that the beauty of the image is that of the prototype

and that the original is palpably discerned in its copy. In the same way, she who says 'I am for my kinsman, and my kinsman is for me' asserts that she is conformed to Christ, that she has recovered her very own beauty, the primordial blessedness of the human race, that is, to be arrayed in a beauty that conforms to the image and likeness of the first, the sole, and the true beauty.

The same thing comes about with a mirror when – granted that it is put together with skill and in conformity with its function – it displays in itself on its clear surface the exact imprint of the face it reflects. In just this way, the soul, when she has put herself together in a way suited to her function and cast off every material defilement, has graven into herself the pure look of the inviolate beauty. Hence the life-endued and choice-endowed mirror has this word to say: 'Since I focus upon the face of my kinsman with my entire being, the entire beauty of his form is seen in me.'

Paul openly echoes these words when he says that he, who has died to the world, lives to God and that Christ alone lives in him (Gal. 2:20). For one who says, 'To me, to live is Christ' (Phil 1:21), by this statement affirms for all the world to hear that in him not a single one of the human and material passions is alive, not pleasure or grief, not anger or fear or cowardice or agitation or vanity or rashness, not vengefulness or envy, nor yet a vindictive disposition or love of money, of glory, or of honours, or anything else that stains the soul by means of some attachment. But he alone is mine who is none of these things. I have scraped off everything that is discerned as alien to that nature of his, and I have in me nothing such as is not found in him. For that reason, 'To me, to live is Christ' – or, in the words of the Bride, 'I am for my kinsman, and my kinsman is for me,' he who is sanctification and purity, and incorruptibility, and light, and truth, and all the like.

- As you grow in holiness you are not becoming less yourself; you are becoming more like the self you were made to be.

70.

Richard Sibbes on the Song of Songs 6:3

I am my beloved's and my beloved is mine;
he grazes among the lilies.

Richard Sibbes (see #2) describes our relationship with Christ
as a 'mystical marriage'. He uses the word 'mystical' because
it's not a literal marriage, but neither it is simply a picture: the
church really is joined to Christ in a covenant of love. First and
foremost, in this union we get Christ Himself. But we also get
all that belongs to Christ (just as a wife shares the privileges
and property of her husband).

'I am my beloved's and my beloved is mine.' The words themselves
are a passionate expression of long-looked-for consolation. These
words come from a full and large heart, expressing the union
and communion between Christ and the church, especially after
a desertion.

First, this union is a union of persons, which comes before all
comfort and communion of graces. Christ's person is ours, and
our persons are his. For, as it is in marriage, if the person of the
husband be not the wife's, his goods are not hers, nor his titles
of honour. For these all come to her because his person is hers.
For he has passed over the right of his own body and person
to his wife, as she has passed over all the right of herself to her
husband. So it is in this mystical marriage. That which entitles
us to a communion of graces is the union of persons between
Christ and his church. 'I am my beloved's and my beloved
himself is mine.' Indeed nothing else will bring contentment to

a Christian's heart. We would not care so much for heaven itself if we had not Christ there. The sacrament, word, and comforts, why do we esteem them? Because they come from Christ, and as because they lead to Christ. It is an adulterous and base affection to love anything severed from Christ.

Now from this union of persons comes a communion of all other things. 'I am my beloved's and my beloved is mine.' If Christ himself is mine then all is mine. What he has done, what he has suffered, is mine; the benefit of all is mine. What he has is mine. His prerogatives and privileges to be the Son of God, and heir of heaven, all is mine. Why? Because he himself is mine. Union is the foundation of communion. So it is here with the church, 'I am my beloved's.' My person is his, my life is his, to glorify him, and to lay it down when he will. My goods are his, my reputation his. I am content to sacrifice all for him. I am his, all mine is his. So you see there is union and communion mutually between Christ and his church. The original and spring is Christ's uniting and communicating himself to his church first. The spring is the beginning of the stream. What does a stream or cistern contain that it is has not received from the spring? We love him because he loved us first (1 John 4:19) ...

'He grazes among the lilies.' The church here shows where Christ feeds. He both feeds his church among the lilies, and delights himself to be there ... Therefore let us come to this sweet food of our souls with hungry appetites and thankful hearts, that God has given us the best comforts of his word, and fed us with the sweet comforts of the sacraments, as a seal of the word.

- We can offer everything we have to Christ because Christ gives everything He has to us.

71.

Charles Spurgeon on the Song of Songs 6:4

You are beautiful as Tirzah, my love,
lovely as Jerusalem,
awesome as an army with banners.

Here the beloved (Christ) describes His bride (the church).
Charles Spurgeon (see #7) says the 'banner' to which we rally
is the crucified Christ. The cross of Christ is 'awesome' (in
the sense of filling God's enemies with awe) because Christ's
atoning work on the cross releases us from the grip of sin, and
because the cross fills weak saints with courage.

It is evident that the Divine Bridegroom gives his bride a high
place in his heart. Moreover, even to him there is not only a
beauty of a soft and gentle kind in her, but a majesty, a dignity,
in her holiness, in her earnestness, in her consecration, which
makes even him say of her that she is 'awesome as an army with
banners'. She is every inch a queen ...

But why an *army with banners*? Is not this, first of all, for
distinction? How shall we know to which king an army belongs
unless we can see the royal standard? ...

But why is it *awesome* because of its banners? I believe the
great banner of the Christian church is the uplifted Saviour
(John 12:32). Look at its exterior, and it does not possess in
itself, naturally, the elements of strength according to ordinary
reckoning. But here lies its strength: that each of the true members
of the church are of the royal seed. They are the weakness of
God, but they are stronger than men. He has determined with

the things that are not, to bring to nought the things that are (1 Cor. 1:28) ... The chief glory and majesty of the church lies mainly in the banner which she carries.

What cause for terror is there in the banner? We reply: the enemies of Christ dread the cross because they know what the cross has done. Wherever the crucified Jesus has been preached, false systems have tottered to their downfall. The most violent rage is excited by the doctrine of the atonement, a rage in which the first cause for wrath is fear. The terribleness of the church lies in her banners because those banners put strength into her. Drawing near to the standard of the cross, the weakest soldier becomes strong. He who might have played the coward becomes a hero when the precious blood of Jesus is felt with power in his soul. Martyrs are born and nurtured at the cross. It is the blood of Jesus which is the life-blood of self-denial. We can die because our Saviour died. The crucified One must conquer. The hands nailed to the wood must sway the sceptre of all kingdoms. In Christ preached lies the battle-axe and weapons of war with which the Lord will work out his everlasting decrees ...

So let us ask ourselves: Am I a soldier? I may have entered the church, but am I really a soldier? Do I fight? Do I endure hardship? Am I a mere lie-a-bed soldier? Am I a soldier who engages in actual fighting for Jesus under his banner? Am I in any way awesome through being a Christian? Is there enough of Christ about my life to make me like a light in the midst of the darkness?

May your life and mine never be so despicable, but may we convince those who deny the truth that there is power in the gospel of Jesus Christ, and make them confess that they, not having it, are losing a great blessing!

- "The weapons we fight with are not the weapons of the world. On the contrary, they have divine power to demolish strongholds" (2 Cor. 10:4 NIV).

72.

James Durham on the Song of Songs 6:5-7

Turn away your eyes from me,
for they overwhelm me—
Your hair is like a flock of goats
leaping down the slopes of Gilead.
Your teeth are like a flock of ewes
that have come up from the washing;
all of them bear twins;
not one among them has lost its young.
Your cheeks are like halves of a pomegranate
behind your veil.

In the following contribution, James Durham (see #13) highlights the fact that the beloved largely repeats in 6:5-7 what he said in 4:1-3. That's because believers often fear Christ's attitude to them has changed, particularly after they've sinned. But the affections of Christ towards His bride never change. So the primary reason we read God's Word and hear it preached is not to learn new information, but to be reassured of Christ's love.

The particulars of his commendation of her in verses 5-7 are set down in the same words in 4:1-3 ... Consider the reason for repeating them and using the same words. It's this. Although he commended her formerly in these expressions, yet considering her foul slip in chapter 5, and his withdrawal on the back of it, she might think that he had other thoughts of her now, and that these privileges and promises which she had reason to claim before, did not belong to her now, and therefore she could not comfortably plead an interest in them now as before ...

From this we may observe, just as believers are liable to slip and fail in their duty, so are they liable to suspect Christ to change his attitude towards them because of their failings. They are apt from their own fickleness and changeability to assume him to be changeable as well, and to refuse comfort from all previous evidences and intimations of his love, and from all the words that have comforted them, till they be restored and set right again.

But our Bridegroom is constant in his affection to his Bride, continuing still the same. And, just as he is the most free forgiver of wrongs to his own, so he is the most full forgetter of them, when his people return in repentance. And therefore he continues speaking to her in the same terms as before without any alteration, as if no such wrong on her side had been committed. Renewing repentance and faith after failings, puts believers in that same relationship with Christ as they had before, with the same claims to his love, and the same privileges and comforts, even as if such failings and misconduct had never happened. Our Lord Jesus would have his people confirmed and strengthened in the faith of the constancy of his love, the unchangeableness of their interest, and the resulting privileges. And seeing he thus loves his people, he allows them to believe it.

It is not easy to fix and imprint Christ's words on the hearts of believers, and to get them affected by them. Therefore often both promises and duties must be repeated. What was once spoken must be again repeated for their good, especially after a slip. The same word needs to be made living again, and fresh to their relish, as the Lord does here. Unless Christ speak and make the word living, the sweetest word, even that which once possibly has been made living to a believer, will not savour, but will want its relish and lustre, until he repeat it.

- Is there a sin that haunts your memory? Christ is 'the most free forgiver' and 'the most full forgetter' when His people return in repentance.

73.

John Gill on the Song of Songs 6:8-9

There are sixty queens and eighty concubines,
and virgins without number.
My dove, my perfect one, is the only one,
the only one of her mother,
pure to her who bore her.
The young women saw her and called her blessed;
the queens and concubines also, and they praised her.

'She's the only one for me,' a man might say today of his beloved. And the church is 'the only one' for Christ. Though there are many believers, says John Gill, we are united in one body that we might be the one and only bride of Christ, and the one and only object of His desire. Gill (1697-1771) was an eighteenth-century Baptist minister in London, where he pastored the same church for over fifty years – the church that, a century later, would be led by Charles Spurgeon (see #7).

'My dove, my perfect one, is the only one.' The church is but one body. Just as there are various parts of a human body, and yet only one body, so the church is also one body, even though it is made up of many believers. In the same way there are many sheep in a flock, and yet only one flock under the care of one shepherd. There are many beds in a garden, each with a variety of spices, flowers, herbs and plants in these beds, and yet only one garden. In the same way, though there are many individual congregations, each with a variety of believers, yet there is only one 'assembly of the firstborn who are enrolled in heaven' (Heb. 12:23) ... The Beloved says she is 'the only one of her mother'. By her mother is meant 'the Jerusalem above' who is 'the mother' of all believers. And the church is 'the only one of her mother' because the heavenly Jerusalem has no child other than the church ...

The church has only one Spirit, which operates and influences this body. The same Spirit that dwells in the head, Christ, dwells in his body, the church. And the same Spirit that dwells in the body as a whole, dwells in each of its members. For though there are a diversity of gifts and various graces, yet there is only one Spirit who distributes them to the members for their use and profit.

The church has only one head and husband, Lord and Saviour. She has only one head, to whom she holds, and from whom she receives life and nourishment, and so increases with the increase of God. The church has only one husband, whom she owns and acknowledges as such, and to whom she is 'betrothed ... as a pure virgin' (2 Cor. 11:2). The church has only one lord, under whose government she is governed, and to whom alone she yields obedience. And the church has only one mediator to whom she looks, and that is, 'the man Christ Jesus' (1 Tim. 2:5).

Though the many members of the church are only one body, united to one head, and operated by one and the same Spirit, its members all enjoy the same privileges. They are built upon one and the same foundation, Christ. They are washed in the same blood. They wear the same righteousness. And they receive from the same fullness, 'grace upon grace' (John 1:16).

The church's members profess one and the same faith. For, just as there is only one Lord, so there is only one faith. The doctrine of grace does not change; it is like its author who is 'the same yesterday and today and forever' (Heb. 13:8). There never was another gospel, nor never will be ...

The members of the church are one in affections, or at least ought to be. Their chief business should be to 'to maintain the unity of the Spirit in the bond of peace' (Eph. 4:3). For this is one end of their calling, the glory of their profession, and a distinguishing characteristic of being the disciples and church of Christ. This unity expresses the fact that she is the only spouse and bride of Christ: 'my dove, my perfect one, is the only one.' Christ says in effect: 'Though other princes may have their sixty queens, eighty concubines and countless virgins to wait upon them, I have only one, and I am delighted with her. I desire no-one but her, for my one is preferable to their many.' And she replies: 'I am my beloved's,' that is, I only belong to him and there is no one else for me.

- 'Be completely humble and gentle; be patient, bearing with one another in love. Make every effort to keep the unity of the Spirit through the bond of peace' (Eph. 4:2-3 NIV). What might this look like for you this week?

74.

Matthew Henry on the Song of Songs 6:10

'Who is this who looks down like the dawn,
beautiful as the moon, bright as the sun,
awesome as an army with banners?'

The people of God have always been a light to the nations. Matthew Henry (see #20) says the light cast by Israel in the Old Testament was like the light of the moon when compared to the sunlight spread by the church, now that a new day has dawned with the coming of Christ. The church is also like an army, fighting under the banner of the gospel.

Christians are, or should be, the lights of the world. The church of the Patriarchs looked 'forth as the morning' (KJV) when the promise of the Messiah was first made known, and the dayspring from on high visited this dark world (Luke 1:78). The Jewish church was 'beautiful as the moon'. The ceremonial law was an imperfect light for it shone by reflection. It was changing as the moon, did not make day, nor had 'the sun of righteousness' yet risen (Mal. 4:2). But the Christian church is 'bright as the sun', and exhibits 'a great light' to 'those who dwelt in a land of deep darkness' (Isa. 9:2).

In its rise, the gospel-kingdom looks 'like the dawn' after a dark night. It is revealing (Job 38:12-13), and very welcome. It looks forth pleasantly as a clear morning. But it is small in its beginnings, and scarcely perceptible at first. It is, at the best, while in this world, merely 'beautiful as the moon', which shines with a borrowed light, which has her changes and eclipses, and her spots too, and, even when full, does but rule by night. But when the kingdom of grace is perfected in the kingdom of glory then it will be 'bright as the sun', the church 'clothed with the sun' (Rev. 12:1), with Christ 'the sun of righteousness' (Mal. 4:2). Those that love God will then be 'like the sun as he rises in his might' (Judg. 5:31; Matt. 13:43). They shall shine in inexpressible glory, and that which is perfect will then come so that there shall be no darkness, no spots (Isa. 30:26).

The beauty of the church and of believers is not only amiable, but 'awesome as an army with banners'. The church, in this world, is 'as an army', as the camp of Israel in the wilderness. Its state is militant; it is in the midst of enemies and is engaged in a constant conflict with them. Believers are soldiers in this army. It has its 'banners': the gospel of Christ is an ensign (Isa. 11:12), the love of Christ (Song 2:4). It is marshalled, and kept in order and under discipline. It is 'awesome' to its enemies as Israel in the wilderness was (Exod. 15:14). When Balaam saw Israel encamped according to their tribes, with their standards, with colours displayed, he said, 'How lovely are your tents, O Jacob' (Num. 24:5). When the church preserves her purity, she secures her honour and victory. When she is 'beautiful as the moon' and 'bright as the sun', she is truly great and formidable.

- 'Let your light shine before others, so that they may see your good works and give glory to your Father who is in heaven' (Matt. 5:16).

75.

George Burrowes on the Song of Songs 6:11-13

She: *I went down to the nut orchard*
to look at the blossoms of the valley,
to see whether the vines had budded,
whether the pomegranates were in bloom.
Before I was aware, my desire set me
among the chariots of my kinsman, a prince.
Others: *Return, return, O Shulammite,*
return, return, that we may look upon you.
He: *Why should you look upon the Shulammite,*
as upon a dance before two armies?

Sometimes we hold Christ at arm's length; sometimes Christ withdraws a sense of His presence to stimulate our desire for Him. But, says George Burrowes (see #14), even then, His love for us does not change. He is ready to come to us because He still desires to be with us. He is, as it were, ready to climb into His chariot and race towards His returning bride.

In verses 11-13 the beloved shows the spouse his feelings during his withdrawal. He says that when he left her in chapter 5:6 it was not in anger, but with kindly feelings and unabated love. He withdraws to his favourite place in the garden, there to occupy himself until such time as she might feel her unkindness, and seek again his presence. He was ready to welcome her return at any moment ...

This love is our life, the very spring of our being. Happy for us that its exercise towards us by our Lord, does not depend on our merit and watchfulness. Like the power which keeps the heart beating unconsciously without any act of our will, this divine love, which began towards us while dead in sins, even before our being, continues to follow and bless us, even when unmindful of its source or its existence, and when unkindly forsaking the Redeemer. Even under neglect and repulse, Jesus turns away from us without anger; and leaves us until such time as we feel our unkindness, and seek again his presence and grace.

Before I was aware of it, my soul made me like 'the chariots of Amminadab' (verse 12 KJV). While an explanation of this phrase is difficult, perhaps impossible, the general meaning seems clear ... The beloved means to say that after thus withdrawing from the spouse without anger, with chastened affections – almost unconsciously, before he was aware of it, his soul was filled with the desire to meet her again, a desire so strong that it would have carried him to her arms with a swiftness that could be illustrated by nothing more appropriately than rapid, smooth-rolling chariots.

Such is the feeling of Jesus towards us, even when his presence is withdrawn, and the light of his countenance no longer felt. He changes not. When obliged by our neglect to turn away from us, he carries with him the same ardour of love that he manifested to us in our happiest hours of duty and affection. When our love has grown cold, and our feet are wandering on the dark mountains, or our souls slumbering in the indifference of fleshly security, he still has an affection which makes him ready to come and meet us at any moment, with the swiftness of chariots. Though seeing it necessary for our good to hide his face, and even afflict us, he has all the while this strong yearning toward us. And every act towards us, however painful, has lying behind it in his heart this deep affection and tenderness ...

The spirit of verse 13 implies that the spouse was in the eyes of the Beloved an object causing more pleasure than such scenes as these. With a delight of which this is the best, though faint, resemblance does Jesus view the sanctified soul, and the innumerable multitude who make up his redeemed Church. Of all his varied works of creation, this is to him the most glorious ...

We may therefore be comforted by keeping in mind the four things stated here concerning the departure of Jesus from us when grieved away by our neglect: 1. He withdraws, not in anger, but in love. 2. He never ceases to feel the strongest desire to return to us. 3. He earnestly invites us to return. 4. And he continues still to view us with unabated love, even with greater pleasure than the angels, the hosts seen by Jacob at Mahanaim.

- 'Jesus Christ is the same yesterday and today and forever' (Heb. 13:8).

76.

Madame Guyon on the Song of Songs 7:1-7

How beautiful are your feet in sandals,
O noble daughter!
Your rounded thighs are like jewels,
the work of a master hand.
Your navel is a rounded bowl
that never lacks mixed wine.
Your belly is a heap of wheat,
encircled with lilies.
Your two breasts are like two fawns,
twins of a gazelle.
Your neck is like an ivory tower.
Your eyes are pools in Heshbon,
by the gate of Bath-rabbim.
Your nose is like a tower of Lebanon,
which looks toward Damascus.
Your head crowns you like Carmel,
and your flowing locks are like purple;
a king is held captive in the tresses.
How beautiful and pleasant you are,
O loved one, with all your delights!
Your stature is like a palm tree,
and your breasts are like its clusters.

In the following excerpt Madame Guyon links each part of this description of the bride to a feature of the church. She highlights the way we can move towards deeper intimacy with God while enjoying rest in Him. Then she speaks of the way the church gives birth and nourishes children (converts). The church is lovely in all these ways because of her connection to her head, Christ. She is like a mirror that reflects back the beauty of Christ. Madame Guyon (1648-1717) was an influential French mystic whose ideas on prayer and grace brought her into conflict with the French Catholic Church.

'How beautiful are your feet in sandals, O noble daughter!' O child of God! Your steps are beautiful both within and outside.

Her inner steps are beautiful because she may continually advance towards God without ceasing to rest in God. The enchanting beauty of this advance is that it is a true rest, a rest which does not hinder her progress, and a true progress which does not interfere with her rest. On the contrary, the greater the rest in God, the greater the progress towards God, and the swifter the progress, the more tranquil the rest.

Her steps outside in public are also full of beauty. For she is well ordered, being obedient to the will of God and subject to his providence. Every step her feet takes is in the will of God, from which they never depart ...

'Your navel is a rounded bowl.' By the *navel* is meant the capacity of the soul to receive from God, or the passive disposition which is extended towards God, since she has been received into God. This is not only so she can receive communications of God's presence, but also so she may conceive and bring forth many children for Jesus Christ ...

It would be a small matter for the spouse to bear children for the Bridegroom if he gave her nothing for their nourishment. So the Bridegroom goes on to speak of her breasts, to show that she is not only a mother, but a nurse. In fact, she has the abundant nourishment for her children. For her breasts are always full, even though they are constantly being emptied. Though her children make demands on them, they do not decrease. On the contrary, their fulness increases with the graces they provide, so that the measure of their supply is the measure of their fulness ...

Christ sees in his spouse his own perfections reflected back as in a true mirror. And, enchanted with his own beauty as he contemplates it in her, Christ exclaims:

'How beautiful and pleasant you are.' How glorious is my beauty in you! You are all my delight, just as I am the delight of my Father. For, as you reflect me, as if in a costly mirror which produces no distortion in the objects held before it, so you give me infinite pleasure. You are beautiful and enchanting, for you are clothed with all my perfections. But if you are my delight, I am also yours, and we share together in our pleasure.

- Hear the voice of Christ speaking to you today: 'How beautiful and pleasant you are, O loved one, with all your delights!'

77.

Richard Sibbes on the Song of Songs 7:8-10

I say I will climb the palm tree
and lay hold of its fruit.
Oh may your breasts be like clusters of the vine,
and the scent of your breath like apples,
and your mouth like the best wine.
She: *It goes down smoothly for my beloved,*
gliding over lips and teeth.
I am my beloved's,
and his desire is for me.

The sexual imagery of these verses, says Richard Sibbes (see #2), points to the passionate desire of Christ for communion with His people. So, if we feel spiritually dry, we should look for the cause in ourselves. Sibbes spotlights a couple of possibilities. It might be the company we're keeping (or the influences that are shaping our outlook), or it might be a neglect of spiritual duties (like Bible reading, prayer, or fellowship with believers).

Christ desires a nearer and nearer communion with his church. Even as the true soul that is touched with the Spirit desires nearer and nearer communion with Christ, so Christ seeks nearer and nearer communion with his spouse by all sanctified means. Christ has never enough of the soul. He would have them more and more open to him. Our hearts are for Christ, who has the heaven of heavens, and the soul of a believing Christian for himself to dwell in. He does not content himself to be in heaven alone, but he will have our hearts. He knocks here, waits, speaks friendly and lovingly, with such sweet words, 'My love, my dove' (Song 5:2).

The time of this life is only the time of the marriage engagement, yet during this time there are many exchanges of mutual love between him and his spouse, a desire for mutual communion on both sides. Christ desires a deeper place in his church's heart and affection, that he might dwell there. And likewise there is a similar desire in the church when she is in a right frame of mind. So if there is any estrangement between Christ and a person's soul – a soul that has tasted how good the Lord is – let that person not blame Christ for it, for Christ does not delight in estrangement ...

Therefore look for the cause of this estrangement in your own self. See whether you have cast yourself imprudently into company that is not fit to be consulted, in whom the Spirit is not present, and who cannot do us any good. Evil company is a great dampener, by which a Christian loses much of their comfort, especially that intimate communion with God. In this way we can fall into complacency.

Or discontinuing our religious exercises causes Christ to withdraw himself. He no longer makes love to our souls when we neglect the means of grace, and discontinue holy exercises, and religious company; when we do not stir up the graces of God's Spirit. When we are negligent in this way, it is no wonder that Christ makes no more love to our souls since we are no longer valuing as we should the communion that should be between the soul and Christ. 'Whom have I in heaven but you?' and 'Your steadfast love is better than life,' says the psalmist (Ps. 73:25; 63:3). When we prize not this, it is just for Christ to make himself strange to us. Where love is not esteemed, it is estranged, and for a while hides itself.

So in these, along with failings, we may find the reason for the estrangement between Christ and the soul, for certainly the cause is not in him. For we see here, he uses all means to be welcomed by a Christian soul. You know what he says to the church of Laodicea: 'Behold, I stand at the door and knock' (Rev. 3:20). So here in the Song he stands and knocks: 'My beloved is knocking' (Song 5:2). Therefore search your own hearts to see if there be deadness and desertion of spirit. Lay the blame upon yourselves, and enter into a search of your own conduct to see what the cause may be.

- 'Christ has never enough of the soul. He would have them more and more open to him.' Can you feel Christ's desire for you?

78.

Charles Spurgeon on the Song of Songs 7:11-13

Come, my beloved,
let us go out into the fields
and lodge in the villages;
let us go out early to the vineyards
and see whether the vines have budded,
whether the grape blossoms have opened
and the pomegranates are in bloom.
There I will give you my love.
The mandrakes give forth fragrance,
and beside our doors are all choice fruits,
new as well as old,
which I have laid up for you, O my beloved.

In the imagery of the Song of Songs, the bride suggests they go together to inspect their fields. Charles Spurgeon (see #7) sees this as a picture of self-examination. It is right from time to time, he says, to reflect on whether we are bearing spiritual fruit. But the main point he makes is that we should do this *with Christ*, that is, in the light of His saving work and gracious love. If we simply evaluate ourselves against the law, then we will despair. Instead, we must always evaluate ourselves as those who are in Christ.

In these verses *the Church desires to practice self- examination*. She would go and see whether the vine flourishes, and whether the tender grape appears. But it is self-examination *with him* … Self-examination is a most desirable and important business, but every believer should desire to have communion with Christ while he is attending to it ...

No trader who wishes to succeed would neglect to keep their books. In soul-business, it is of no use taking anything for granted where there are so many temptations to self-deception in our own hearts ...

Yet self-examination is *beset with difficulties*. If you take the law of Moses with you when you examine yourself, you will fall into despair. Brothers and sisters, remember to take Jesus with you, and not Moses, lest you dishonour the grace of God. I do not ask, 'Am I perfect?' That is the question the law of Moses would suggest. I ask, 'Am I perfect in Christ Jesus?' That is a very different matter. I do not put like this, 'Am I without sin naturally?' But like this, 'Have I been washed in the fountain opened for sin and for uncleanness?' (Zech. 13:1) It is not, 'Am I in myself well-pleasing to God?' but, 'Am I accepted in the Beloved?' When a believer looks at their love they say, 'Surely I am condemned, for my love is so cold.' But if they had looked at *Christ's* love, they would have said, 'No, never shall I be condemned; for many waters cannot quench his love, neither can the floods drown it, and, loving me as he does, he will never condemn me, nor cast me away.'

I do not want you to look at Christ so as to think less of your sin, but to think more of it. For you never see sin to be so evil as when you see the suffering which Christ endured on its behalf. But I do desire you, dear friends, never to look at sin apart from the Saviour. If you gaze at the disease and forget the remedy, you will be driven to despair. If you look at the gathering gangrene and forget the all-gracious Surgeon who is able to remove it, you may well lie down and die. If you see your own emptiness and poverty, and forget his fulness, you will never glorify his name. Examine yourselves, but let it be in the light of Calvary – not by the blazing fires of Sinai's lightning, but by the milder radiance of the Saviour's griefs.

Am I resting upon you, Son of God? Are your wounds my hiding place? Have your nails nailed me to your cross? Has your spear pierced my heart, and broken it with grief for sin? And am I now crucified with you to the world, buried with you as to the power of sin, risen with you to newness of life, and, like yourself, waiting for the day of manifestation when sin, death, and hell shall be trodden under foot, and Jesus shall be all in all?

- Robert Murray M'Cheyne famously said: 'For every look at yourself, take ten looks at Christ. He is altogether lovely ... Live much in the smiles of God ... Let your soul be filled with a heart-ravishing sense of the sweetness and excellency of Christ and all that is in him.'

79.

George Burrowes on the Song of Songs 8:1

*Oh that you were like a brother to me
who nursed at my mother's breasts!
If I found you outside, I would kiss you,
and none would despise me.*

The bride wishes her betrothed were her brother, so she can kiss him in public without offending the social norms of her day. George Burrowes (see #14) sees this as a picture of the soul longing to enjoy the intimacy with Christ that one day we will enjoy in heaven.

This verse expresses the desire that everything hindering the full and perfect interchange of affection between Jesus and our soul might be removed.

We wish it were possible to enjoy his love to us and express our love to him, as we shall be able to do in heaven. While we now may long for stronger displays of his love, and long to give stronger evidence of our love to him, we accept the present state of things, because we feel it would be inappropriate and indeed impossible to display those overpowering exhibitions of love which belong to heaven. But this does not stop us feeling that, if he thought it best, we would rejoice now in heavenly raptures. For in heaven we shall be able to speak of his love in the strongest language, and give expression to it in the most exalted praise, without danger of exposing ourselves to the contempt of the world. There, our fellowship and communion with him shall be far more intimate and endearing than was possible on earth. So the language of this verse expresses the real feeling of the pious heart.

As it is, nominal Christians often accuse us of being inappropriate or excessive, even though our affections are perfectly free from fanaticism, and spring from the overflowing influence of the Holy Spirit on the heart. In this present world, we are unable to feel as we would wish we could feel towards our Lord. And we cannot speak of him as we would wish to speak of him. We cannot interact with him as we would wish to interact with him. We are prevented by our position among those who are unable to understand these things; by the remaining corruptions of our own hearts; by the specific duties now resting on us; and by the relationship Jesus must necessarily have towards us in the present world.

Well may the wearied heart, with so many obstructions between us and the object of our love, desire that they may be removed. Well may we wish our relationship with Christ to be transformed with the power to perfectly satisfy our affection for him.

- Perhaps you wish you enjoyed a deeper relationship with Christ, with a greater sense of His presence. Then take heart: one day your wish will come true!

80.

Samuel Rutherford on the Song of Songs 8:2-3

*I would lead you and bring you
into the house of my mother—
she who used to teach me.
I would give you spiced wine to drink,
the juice of my pomegranate.
His left hand is under my head,
and his right hand embraces me!*

Using poetic hyperbole, in the following excerpt Samuel
Rutherford (see #11) says to know something of the glory of
Christ is heavenly, but not to enjoy it for a period is like a
taste of hell. So he longs for a greater experience of Christ.
That experience is something Rutherford can never adequately
convey in words, just as a *description* of honey can never be
better than the *taste* of honey. All the troubles of this life shrink
when compared to the joy of knowing Christ; they cannot take
that joy away.

What heaven can there be more like hell than to desire, and
pine, and swoon for Christ's love, and not to have it? Is not
this hell and heaven woven through together? Is not this pain
and joy, sweetness and sadness, to be in one web, the one the
weft, the other the warp? Therefore, I would that Christ would
let us meet and join together, *the soul and Christ in each other's
arms*. Oh what meeting is like this, to see ugliness and beauty,
contemptibleness and glory, baseness and highness, even a soul
and Christ, kiss each other!

When all is said and done, I may be wearied in speaking and writing, but how far am I from the right expression of Christ or his love! I can neither speak nor write feeling, nor tasting, nor smelling. Come feel, and smell, and taste Christ and his love, and you shall call it more than can be spoken. To write how sweet is the honeycomb is not so lovely as to eat and suck the honeycomb. One night's rest in a bed of love with Christ will say more than a heart can think, or tongue can utter.

Neither need we fear crosses, nor sigh and be sad for anything that is on this side of heaven, if we have Christ. Our crosses will never draw blood from the joy of the Holy Spirit, and peace of conscience. Our joy is laid up in such a high place that temptations cannot climb up to take it down. This world may boast against Christ, but they dare not strike. Or, if they strike, they break their arm in fetching a stroke upon a rock.

O that we could put our treasures in Christ's hand, and give him our gold to keep, and our crown. Strive to push through the thorns of this life, to be at Christ. Do not lose sight of him in this cloudy and dark day. Sleep with him in your heart in the night. Do not learn from the world how to serve Christ, but ask Christ himself to show the way. For the world is a false copy and a lying guide to follow.

- 'I count everything as loss because of the surpassing worth of knowing Christ Jesus my Lord' (Phil. 3:8).

81.

James Durham on the Song of Songs 8:4

I adjure you, O daughters of Jerusalem,
that you not stir up or awaken love until it pleases.

We so easily grow lazy in the pursuit of Christ, says James Durham (see #13) in the following excerpt. So we need to keep stirring up our hearts. (That's one reason why God has given the Song of Songs.) We cannot manufacture or demand experiences of Christ. A felt sense of His presence and love is something He gives as He sees best. But we can do everything in our power to ensure nothing hinders our experience of Him.

It is a difficult piece of work to keep the heart tender and watchful so that it is ready to welcome, even when Christ is present. The strongest believer will require one exhortation after another, and all will have enough to do, to make themselves watchfully tender in keeping Christ. There is so much laziness in the hearts of even the best, and there is so great need to stir them up to renew their watchfulness. When the heart has had frequent proofs of its own neglect of Christ, there is the more need to be serious in preventing it from happening again. There is nothing that a kindly and loving believer will have more indignation at, whether in himself or others, than that Christ should be provoked, and thereby forced to withdraw. This they cannot abide, 'Why,' she says, 'will you stir him up?'

Those who enjoy Christ's presence will not be insistent with him, not demanding that a sense of his presence continues, even though they love it. Instead, they will be insistent with themselves, that they do not provoke him by their sin to withdraw before he please. Communion with Christ is an active exercise for the believer. We are always active so that we never stand still in idleness. If a soul is waiting for Christ, then they are breathing out, 'Oh that you were like a brother to me' and so on (Song 8:1-3), and seeking to find him. If a soul is enjoying Christ, then they are endeavouring to keep and welcome him. We are always taken up with one of these activities. Believers are either *seeking* until they obtain, or *watching* that they may welcome what they have attained.

- 'For God alone, O my soul, wait in silence' (Ps. 62:5).

82.

Thomas Boston on the Song of Songs 8:5

Who is that coming up from the wilderness,
leaning on her beloved?
Under the apple tree I awakened you.
There your mother was in labour with you;
there she who bore you was in labour.

Just as Israel travelled through the wilderness to the promised
land, and the bride travels with her beloved through the
wilderness to her home, so Christians, says Thomas Boston
(see #17), travel through the wilderness of this world to their
home in glory. The last and literal step is made at death. But
our souls make this movement every time we turn away from
worldliness, and opt instead to be heavenly-minded. We do
this by leaning on Christ, just as the bride leans for support
on her beloved.

Here we have an account of the Christian life ... By the wilderness
is meant the world with a plain eye to the Israelites coming
through the wilderness to Canaan. Canaan is a type of heaven,
so the wilderness is a type of the world ... She is travelling on
her road with her betrothed husband, namely, Christ. The place
she is going from is the wilderness-world; the place she is going
to is her Bridegroom's Father's house ... This is what in New
Testament language is called the life of faith, for that is the
spiritual leaning of the soul ...

Her going away up from the wilderness with her betrothed
Husband is a going away in heart and affections. It is the soul's

motion heavenwards in this life, the last step of which is made at death. It is a gracious frame of heart shining forth in a holy, tender and heavenly walk. Every step in the way of holiness – in mortification, vivification, and contempt of the world – is a step homeward to Christ's Father's house ...

As soon as a soul is espoused to Christ, it is loosed from the world. Its taking of him is a letting go of this world (Matt. 13:44). The unbeliever hugs and embraces this world as his inheritance, and pursues it as the main thing. But when he closes with Christ he says, 'You are my portion,' and the esteem of the world sinks (Lam. 3:24; Phil. 3:8) ... The soul betrothed to Christ, being loosed from the world, is set in motion heavenwards, away from the world. He has a low estimate of the world's wisdom and a holy contempt of the world's good things ...

The way to get up from the wilderness-world to the heavenly Canaan is always to go leaning on Jesus Christ by faith. God says in effect, 'Poor souls, you can never of yourselves make your way up through the wilderness. But I freely give you a strong one to lean on. Take him and welcome.' Therefore the soul takes hold of Christ to that end. The soul believes the gospel offer or promise as made to itself, saying in effect, 'He is mine by the free offer made to me.' This implies the heart's consent to take him, and so the betrothals are made (1 John 5:11) ... The Father has appointed the Mediator for this very end, so he may bring many children to glory ... So if you want to go up from the wilderness of this world to the heavenly Canaan, go leaning on Jesus Christ.

1. Go leaning on Christ for light to know your duty (Prov. 3:5). He is the great Prophet and Teacher. As the Israelites followed the cloud in the wilderness, close your own eyes that you may be guided by his word and Spirit.

2. Go leaning on Christ for strength to perform your duty (Phil. 3:13). It will not be your weak hands that will work the work, nor your feeble knees that will perform the journey. The

strength must come from him who is the Head, and you must go on borrowed legs.

3. Go leaning on Christ for acceptance, and the happy outcome of your journey (Eph. 1:6). It is through him alone that any step in the Lord's way can be accepted, and by him alone we can be brought into the eternal rest.

- Every step in the way of holiness – every time we put sin to death or reject worldliness – is another step homeward.

83.

John Flavel on the Song of Songs 8:6

Set me as a seal upon your heart,
as a seal upon your arm,
for love is strong as death,
jealousy is fierce as the grave.
Its flashes are flashes of fire,
the very flame of the LORD.

There is nothing more precious, says John Flavel (see #67), than to be confident that Christ loves us. If we try to do this by assessing ourselves, then the evidence is mixed, and every sin throws us into despair. But, if we look to Christ, we see His love for us displayed in His wounds. It is faith in Christ and His work on the cross that brings assurance. If we are struggling to believe this, then we can ask God to strengthen our faith.

There is nothing in this world which true Christians more earnestly desire than to be well assured and satisfied of the love of Jesus Christ to their souls ... It is the heart's ease; the very sabbath and sweet repose of the soul ...

Thousands of poor Christians would part with all they possess in this world to enjoy it, but it flies from them. The life that most of them live is a life between hopes and fears, for their share in Christ is doubtful to them. Sometimes they are encouraged when they sense the workings of grace. Then all is dashed again by the contrary stirrings and workings of their own corruptions. Sometimes the sun shines clearly, but then the heavens are clouded again. But the assured Christian is at rest from those tormenting fears and jealousies of which the text speaks that are as cruel as the grave, and as insufferable as coals of fire in a person's heart. He can take Christ into the arms of faith, and say, 'My beloved is mine, and I am his.' 'Return, O my soul, to your rest; for the LORD has dealt bountifully with you' (Ps. 116:7) ...

Do you want to be secure in Christ's love to you, and that you are set as a seal upon his heart? Then behold him as he is here represented to you, wounded for your iniquities, sacrificed to the wrath of God, for your peace, pardon and salvation! O what manner of love is this! Behold how he loved you! If Christ's love draw out yours, your share in his love will be clear, as it shall engage your heart in love to him ...

Next, I advise you to make it the main work and business of this hour to exercise your faith on Jesus Christ. Realize the sufferings of Christ for you, and behold them here represented in the Lord's Supper in a true mirror to the eye of faith. See that bread broken, and that wine poured out? As sure as this is so, Jesus Christ endured the cross and suffered the wrath of the great and terrible God in his soul and in his body upon the cursed tree in the place of poor condemned sinners. Apply the sufferings of Christ this day to your own soul. Believe all this to be done and suffered in your place and for your sake. He did not offer this sacrifice for his own sins, but ours (Isa. 53:9; Heb. 7:27). He was incarnate for you (Isa. 9:6). His death was for you, and in your place (Gal. 3:13). And when he rose from the dead, 'he rose for our justification' (Rom. 4:25). And now that he is in glory at the right hand of God, he is there for us (Heb. 7:25) ...

In a word, pour out your soul to God in heartfelt desires for a sealed and clear interest in his love this day. Tell him it is mercy you value above life; for his steadfast love is better than life (Ps. 63:3). Tell him, you are not able to live with the jealousies and suspicions of his love. You are a torment to yourself while your share in his love abides under a cloud ... O cry to him in the words of this text with the deep sense of the spouse: 'Set me as a seal upon your heart' (which has a most vehement heat), 'as a seal upon your arm, for love is strong as death, jealousy is fierce as the grave. Its flashes are flashes of fire, the very flame of the LORD.'

- 'Let us draw near with a true heart in full assurance of faith, with our hearts sprinkled clean from an evil conscience and our bodies washed with pure water' (Heb. 10:22).

84.

Anne Dutton on the Song of Songs 8:6

Set me as a seal upon your heart,
as a seal upon your arm,
for love is strong as death,
jealousy is fierce as the grave.
Its flashes are flashes of fire,
the very flame of the LORD.

The love of Christ is not only as strong as death; it overcomes death. Christ resolved to do battle with death to win His bride, says Anne Dutton (see #61) in the following excerpt. She then imagines Christ addressing Death personified. Christ invites Death to destroy Him, knowing that in so doing He will destroy Death and liberate His bride.

Though Christ foresaw all the guilt and defilement, all the death and wrath, the Bride would bring on herself by her Fall in the first Adam, yet so great was his love that he resolved to put himself, his great self, in her place. He resolved to take her nature, to stand in her law-place, to bear her sin, and die in her stead so that he might set her free, deliver her from death, and raise her up to perfect life and glory in and with himself forever. He resolved that nothing should separate her from that love-union, nor from any of the glorious fruits of the communion that flows from this union which his great love had ordained. He would die for her rather than lose her irrecoverably in the Fall. When she had deserved death, was under the sentence of death, and must have died eternally, his love, strong as death,

265

endures death for her, even the strong death of the cross, to give her life.

And thus, in his godlike strength, his glorious faithfulness, his infinite and unchangeable love, and in view of those vast depths of misery into which she had plunged herself, he resolved in Old Testament times to do battle with those mighty sufferings he must endure if he were to fetch her from her miseries and conquer all: 'I shall ransom them from the power of Sheol; I shall redeem them from Death. O Death, where are your plagues? O Sheol, where is your sting? Compassion is hidden from my eyes' (Hos. 13:14). It is as if he says:

'O death, you have conquered my Bride. But I will be your plagues. I, who am the Prince of Life, will give myself to your sting. You shall try you strength on me. I will open my heart to your sharpest darts. A thought of parting with my Bride, of leaving her under your conquest, is a much keener dart to wound my heart than any you have in your quiver. And therefore, strike me through, body and soul. And when you have done your worst, and brought me into the dust of death, I will thereby, in the infinite merit of my death, satisfy God's law and justice, and so be your plagues and death. And in the infinity of my life, having conquered you, O death, I will take my Bride into my embraces, and out of your cruel hands. And so, O grave, I'll be your destruction. You have got a legal victory over my Bride. But I'll become your captive. I'll take a lodging with my Bride in the tomb. And, by becoming a captive, I'll be your conqueror. I'll break your bars and gates, and by the power of my endless life I'll set her free. You cannot hold me. I will rise from under your dominion, and raise her up mystically in myself as the foundation of her personal resurrection from under your power at the last day to an endless life and glory with me. When in glorious triumph, I'll be your full and everlasting destruction.'

- '"Death is swallowed up in victory" ... Therefore, my beloved brothers, be steadfast, immovable, always abounding in the work of the Lord, knowing that in the Lord your labour is not in vain' (1 Cor. 15:54, 58)

85.

Charles Spurgeon on the Song of Songs 8:6-7

Set me as a seal upon your heart,
as a seal upon your arm,
for love is strong as death,
jealousy is fierce as the grave.
Its flashes are flashes of fire,
the very flame of the LORD.
Many waters cannot quench love,
neither can floods drown it.
If a man offered for love
all the wealth of his house,
he would be utterly despised.

Christ is physically absent from us, says Charles Spurgeon (see #7) in the following excerpt, but we long for a sense of His spiritual presence. Spurgeon links the 'seal upon your heart' to the names of the Israelite tribes that the high priest wore on his breastplate. It is a sign that Christ our High Priest loves us and cares for us. Just as nothing can restrain death, so nothing can restrain the love of Christ, because His love is as strong as death. Indeed, in Christ these two mighty forces Death and Love – engaged in combat and Love was victorious. So one day Death will have to hand over its prey to Love.

The Bridegroom is not with us. He has left us, gone to prepare a place for us, and is coming again. We are longing for his coming (Song 8:14). Yet before he went it seemed as if his church prayed to him, 'Set me as a seal upon your heart, as a seal upon your arm' (Song 8:6). And this is the cry of the church today, and I trust your cry too, that while he is not present but is absent from you, you may be near to him, and have a sweet consciousness of that blessed fact ...

The high priest of old wore the breastplate with 'the names of the sons of Israel' (Exod. 39:14). These were to indicate that the high priest loved the people, for he bore them on his heart; and that he served the people as a consequence of that love. And I think the prayer of the spouse is just this – she would know once for all that Christ's heart is entirely hers, and that he loves her with the intensity and the very vitality of his being; that his inmost heart, the life-spring of his soul, belongs to her. She longs to see herself supported, sustained, strengthened, defended, preserved, and kept by that same strong arm which put Orion in its place in the sky (Amos 5:8). Can we not, each of us, join the spouse in this prayer? 'Oh, Lord, let me know that my name is engraved on your heart; not only let it be there, but let me know it!' ...

With steadfast steps, death marches over the world. No mountains can restrain the invasion of this all-conquering king. But Christ's love is 'strong as death'. As the sun dissolves the chains of frost, and bids the stream rush on in freedom, though once bound, as if it were in stone, so does this love of Christ. Wherever it comes, it gives life, and joy, and liberty, and snaps the bonds, and has its way ...

Death and Jesus once engaged in a trial of strength; and it was a struggle upon which angels gazed. Jesus – I mean Incarnate Love – at first seemed to shrink before death in Gethsemane (Luke 22:44). You cannot see the brow of his antagonist, but could you have perceived it, death – the invader – was trembling more than Christ – the Invaded. I think I see the flush that crossed the pale face of Death as he thought that he had gained the victory, but Jesus triumphed. Love reigned, while Death lay prostrate at his feet. 'Strong as Death' indeed was Jesus' love, for he swallowed up Death in victory. He did not merely overcome it, but seemed to devour it, to make nothing of it, and put it away once and for all ...

Rest assured that as Death will not give up its prey, so neither will Love. How hard and firm does Death hold its captives! Till that resurrection trumpet sets loose their bonds, none shall go free. And is not Christ's love as strong as this? He shall keep his own. Those who are his, he will never let go. No, when the archangel's trumpet shall dissolve the grasp of death, then shall be heard the cry, 'Father, I desire that they also, whom you have given me, may be with me where I am' (John 17:24). And when Death itself is dead, Love shall prove its eternal strength by taking its captives home ... The love of Christ is like an arrow which has been shot from the bow of destiny; it flies, it flies, and heaven itself cannot change its course.

- 'Neither death nor life ... will be able to separate us from the love of God in Christ Jesus our Lord' (Rom. 8:38-39).

86.

John Gill on the Song of Songs 8:8-10

We have a little sister,
and she has no breasts.
What shall we do for our sister
on the day when she is spoken for?
If she is a wall, we will build on her a battlement of silver,
but if she is a door, we will enclose her with boards of cedar.
I was a wall, and my breasts were like towers;
then I was in his eyes as one who finds peace.

The friends look beyond their own blessing and express their concern for their little sister. They want her to enjoy the same protection that the Bride enjoys (pictured as 'a wall'). John Gill (see #73) sees the 'little sister' as a reference to Gentile believers. Through the mission of the church, they have come to share the protection of Christ. Just as these verses express a determination to protect the *sexual* purity of the sister, so we are to be concerned for the *spiritual* purity of believers.

In verse 10 the Bride describes herself as a wall. For God himself is a wall of fire around his people (Zech. 2:5). Christ's salvation is appointed for walls and bulwarks to them (Isa. 26:1). Faithful ministers and Christian magistrates may also in some sense said to be a wall, being put in place by God for the protection and defence of the church ...

And the church is also a wall built up of living stones (1 Pet. 2:4-5), cemented together in love. By nature the elect of God lie in the same quarry, are taken out of the same pit, and are cut from the same rock as other people. But Christians are separated out by the distinguishing and effective work of grace. They are hewn and fitted by the Spirit of God, and laid by him to create a spiritual house, bound together in the bond of love.

The church is firmly built on Christ, the foundation, which God has laid in Zion (1 Pet. 2:6), and is sure, firm, and lasting, against which the gates of hell can never prevail (Matt. 16:18). This foundation stone will be sufficient to bear up and support the church, and all believers who lay the whole weight of their lives and salvation upon it.

The church is well established in the doctrine of faith. Though it was received in the midst of affliction, yet it was received with much joy in the Holy Spirit (1 Thess. 1:6). And once we have received it, we will not be moved from it - not by all the frowns and flatteries, promises and threatenings, people may make ...

The church is constant and immoveable in her love to Christ. She is a wall that protects against all temptations and insinuations. She is not a door that easily lets into her affections every one that knocks. She loves Christ dearly, and keeps her love undefiled and pure for him. Nothing could separate her from him. The greatest pleasures and profits of life cannot tempt her to desert him; nor can the most dreadful sufferings and torments deter her from expressing her affection to him. She is like a wall that stands invincible and impregnable.

- Are there members of your church whose spiritual purity is being threatened? What could you do to protect them? Pray that, through faith in Christ, they might become a wall against temptation.

87.

James Durham on the Song of Songs 8:11-12

Solomon had a vineyard at Baal-hamon;
he let out the vineyard to keepers;
each one was to bring for its fruit a thousand pieces of silver.
My vineyard, my very own, is before me;
you, O Solomon, may have the thousand,
and the keepers of the fruit two hundred.

James Durham (see #13) sees Solomon and his vineyard as
a picture of Christ and His church. The church is the only
'vineyard' that brings spiritual life and fruit. Christ has
appointed pastors and preachers to look after His church, like
the vine-keepers looking after Solomon's vineyard. It shows
what a 'weighty trust' ministers carry. Their job is to ensure
'Christ's people thrive' and 'produce appropriate fruit'.

By Solomon, we are to understand Christ ... and the vineyard
here is the church (Isa. 5:7) ... Our Lord Jesus has some who
beyond all others are his by specific right and title; and he had
this right to them before ever actually there was a church. This
vineyard belonged to him even before it existed, which could
only be through Father giving the elect to him. Christ has a
notable right to, and propriety in, these elect who are given to
him, so that the vineyard is said to be his. And none of these
can perish without impairing and prejudicing the propriety of
our Lord Jesus.

For there is an old transaction, concerning the salvation of
the elect, between the Father and the Son which is nothing other

than the covenant of redemption. For the Son's claim on some and not on others supposes that some were given to him and accepted by him, as John 17:6 bears out: 'Yours they were, and you gave them to me, and they have kept your word.'

Christ's church or vineyard has the only choice soil in all the world to live in. It is Baal-hamon where they are planted. Though often their outward lot is not desirable, yet their 'lines have fallen ... in pleasant places' (Ps. 16:6).

The second part of the verse concerns Christ's management of his church. He does not tend it by himself without intermediaries, but he lets it out to keepers. As a person having purchased a field or planted a vineyard farms it for a rent, so Christ has thought it good to commit his church to keepers, that is, to watchmen and farmers, that by their ministry, he might in a mediated way promote their edification and salvation, which he accounts his rent ...

Observe, that our Lord Jesus has thought it good to guide the church-militant through intermediaries, by a standing ministry and ordinances ... Although Christ employ ministers, he does not make them masters, but he reserves the propriety of his church to himself, and they are such as must give an account. Though ministers are not masters, yet are they keepers, and have a special trust in the church. They are entrusted with the affairs of Christ's house, to edify his people, which is a trust that no others have committed to them ...

So every minister of the gospel has a weighty trust put on him. Ministers right discharging of this trust may have much influence on whether Christ's people thrive, and whether Christ's gets his 'rent' from among them. So every one of Christ's ministers has the same commission for the same end, and every one of them should endeavour to produce appropriate fruit among God's people ...

- Pray that your pastors and preachers would faithfully discharge their duties, so that Christ's people thrive and produce fruit.

88.

Samuel Rutherford on the Song of Songs 8:13

O you who dwell in the gardens,
with companions listening for your voice;
let me hear it.

In verse 13 the bride has companions who are listening for her voice. Samuel Rutherford (see #11) addresses those companions in the following excerpt. With heartfelt passion, both for Christ and for his readers, he implores us to fall in love with Christ. Rutherford wrote at a time when many gospel ministers (including himself) were not allowed to preach. This is why he speaks of Christ being 'shut out of pulpits and churches'. But even in times of persecution, we can welcome Christ into our hearts. Rutherford's testimony is that, despite all he personally had suffered, Christ is worth it. Nothing this world can offer in any way compares with the delight of knowing Christ and His love.

I wonder that people can abide to be away from Christ. I would esteem myself blessed if I could make an open proclamation, and gather all the people who are living on the earth, Jew and Gentile, and all that shall be born till the blowing of the last trumpet, to flock around Christ, and to stand looking, wondering, admiring, and adoring his beauty and sweetness.

For his fire is hotter than any other fire; his love sweeter than common love; his beauty surpasses all other beauty. When I am heavy and sad, one of his love-looks would do me a world of good. O if you would fall in love with him, how blessed would I be! How glad would my soul be to help you to love him! But among us all, we could not love him enough. He is the Son of the Father's love, and God's delight. The Father's love lies all on him. O that all mankind would fetch all their love and lay it upon him! Invite him and take him home to your houses in the exercise of prayer morning and evening, as I often desired you would.

Do so especially now: let him not be without lodging in your houses when he is shut out of pulpits and churches. If you will be content to take heaven by violence and the wind on your face for Christ and his cross, I am here as one who has some trial of Christ's cross and I can say that Christ was ever kind to me, but he overcomes himself (if I may so speak) in kindness while I suffer for him. I give you my word for it. Christ's cross is not evil as they call it; it is sweet, light, and comfortable. I would not exchange the visitations of love, and the very kisses of Christ's mouth, and my Lord's delightful smiles and loving embraces under my sufferings for him, for a mountain of gold, or for all the honours, courts, and grandeur of velvet churchmen. Christ has the yoke and heart of my love. 'I am my Beloved's, and my Beloved is mine.'

O that you were all betrothed to Christ! O my dearly-beloved in the Lord, I would [that] I could change my voice, and had a tongue tuned by the hands of my Lord, and had the art of speaking of Christ, that I might point out to you the worth, and highness, and greatness, and excellence of that fairest and renowned Bridegroom! I urge you by the mercies of the Lord, by the sighs, tears, and heart's-blood of our Lord Jesus, by the salvation of your poor and precious souls, set off up the mountain that you and I may meet before the Lamb's throne among the congregation of the first-born. The Lord grant that may be the trysting-place, that you and I may put up our hands together, and pluck and eat the apples off the tree of life, and that we may feast together, and drink together of that pure river of the water of life, that comes out from the throne of God and of the Lamb.

- Is there someone you could implore to fall in love with Christ?

89.

Charles Spurgeon on the Song of Songs 8:13

O you who dwell in the gardens,
with companions listening for your voice;
let me hear it.

The beloved (Christ) calls His bride (the church) 'you who
dwell in the gardens'. Charles Spurgeon (see #7) says this
describes both our *enjoyment* and our *employment*. Like Adam
in the Garden of Eden, we are to tend and care for Christ's
garden. Finally, the beloved invites the bride to keep sharing
fellowship with him; he wants to hear her voice. So Spurgeon
invites us to keep praying – not just at one set time in the day,
but with brief prayers throughout the day.

The Song is almost ended. The bride and bridegroom are
about to part for a while. They utter their goodbyes, and
the bridegroom says, 'O you who dwell in the gardens, with
companions listening for your voice; let me hear it.' In other
words, when I am far away from you, fill this garden with my
name, and let your heart commune with me. It is the mystical
word of the church's Lord to his elect one.

He calls her an *inhabitant* of the gardens. He came down
awhile that he might look upon his garden, that he might see
how the vines flourished, and gather lilies. He watered the soil
of his garden with his bloody sweat in Gethsemane, and made
it bear fruit to life. But all this lowly work is over now ...

The title – inhabitant of gardens – is our *employment* as well
as our enjoyment. Adam was put into the garden to keep it

and dress it. If we didn't have our daily tasks to fulfil, we would corrode into rust, and recreation would soon engender corruption. You and I are set in the garden of the church because there is work for us to do which will be beneficial to others and to ourselves as well. Some have to take the broad axe and hew down mighty trees of error; others of a feebler sort can, with a child's hand, train the tendrils of a climbing plant, or drop into its place a tiny seed. One may plant and another may water; one may sow, and another gather fruit. A schoolbook with which to teach the little children may be, for a while, more to our true advantage than a golden harp ...

Brothers, have you found out what you have to do in these gardens? Sisters, have you found out the plants for which you are to care? Speak to him who is the Lord of all true servants, and say to him, 'Show me what you would have me do. Point out, I pray you, the place where I may serve you' ...

Now we come to the pith of the text: *invited fellowship*. 'With companions listening for your voice; let me hear it.' It is beautiful to hear the Beloved say, in effect:

> I am going away from you, and you will see me no more. But I shall see you. Do not forget me. Though you will not hear my voice with your bodily ears, I shall hear your voices. Therefore speak to me. Unseen, I shall feed among the lilies; unperceived, I shall walk the garden in the cool of the day. When you are talking to others, do not forget me. Sometimes we will turn aside, and when you have shut the door, and no eye can see, or ear can hear, then let me hear your voice. It has music in it for my heart, for I died to give you life. Let me hear the voice of your prayer, and praise, and love ...

It is condescending and gracious, and yet how natural it is! How like Christ! Love ever seeks the company of that which it loves. What would a husband say if his wife were seen to be chatty and cheerful to everybody else, but never spoke to him? ... Speak with Jesus Christ, dear friends, in little broken sentences.

The best of Christian fellowship may be carried on in single syllables. When in the middle of business you can whisper, 'My Lord and my God!' You can dart a glance upward, heave a sigh, or let fall a tear, and know that Jesus will hear your voice! When nobody observes the motion of your lips, you may be saying, 'My Beloved, be near me now!'

- Make 'My Beloved, be near me now!' your repeated prayer throughout this day.

90.

Augustus Toplady on the Song of Songs 8:14

Make haste, my beloved,
and be like a gazelle
or a young stag
on the mountains of spices.

The Song of Songs closes with the bride asking the beloved to come to her quickly. Augustus Toplady interprets this as a request by the church for the 'spiritual presence' of Christ. Christ comes to us through the means of grace: through the word and the sacraments. These means of grace, says Toplady, are like a pipe. The pipe matters because it carries the water we need, but what we really want is the water itself. In the same way, just reading your Bible or going to church is not enough. We come to the Word and sacraments thirsty for Christ Himself. The focus must be Christ, for Christ is the altogether lovely one. Hence the prayer, 'Make haste, my beloved'. Toplady (1740-1778) was an Anglican minister, mostly in Devon, England, and a staunch defender of Calvinism. Today he is best known as a hymn-writer (including the hymn 'Rock of Ages').

The church addresses this passage quoted to the Saviour who has redeemed her by his blood. She styles him, 'My beloved'; the object of her supreme affection, and the meritorious procurer of all her happiness. She prays for the manifestations of his spiritual presence; and that those manifestations may be speedy: 'Make haste, my beloved! and be,' in the swiftness of your approach, 'like to a gazelle, or to a young stag, on the mountain of spices!' Rapidly as those lively animals spring from hill to hill, nimbly as they bound, on the fragrant mountains of the east, so swiftly do you lift up the light of your countenance on your waiting people, and cheer them with tokens of your grace and favour that are more reviving to the soul than the odours of spicy mountains to fainting travellers ...

The truly awakened soul considers all the exterior means of grace simply as channels through which grace itself and its comforts are (through God's sovereignty and freeness) communicated to those who hunger and thirst after the righteousness of Jesus Christ. Just as it is not the mere channel of conveyance, but the water conveyed, which satisfies thirst, so the Christian recognises that it is not a bare attendance on outward duties, but the presence of God enjoyed under those duties which nourishes ours souls and renews our strength. The church above and the church below, with whom you have promised to a gracious intimacy, are delighted to hear your voice of love.

'O cause me to hear it! Make me glad with the joy of your salvation! Give me to see the happiness of your chosen, to drink deep of that river, to experience much of that unspeakable fellowship with yourself, which makes glad the city of God both in earth and heaven. Make haste, my beloved, and be like a gazelle or a young stag on the mountains of spices.'

From all this is it is clear that Jesus is the object of his people's love. And whom should we love, if not he who loved us, and gave himself for us? If the bliss even of angels and glorified souls consists greatly in seeing and praising the Son of God, surely to love, to trust, and to celebrate the Friend of Sinners must be a principal ingredient of the happiness of saints not yet made perfect. Solomon, whose experience of grace was lively and triumphant when he wrote this Song of Songs, declares that Christ is 'altogether lovely' (Song 5:16). Other objects may be overrated, and too highly esteemed. But so transcendent and so infinite is the excellence of Christ that he is, and will be to all eternity, more lovely than beloved. Yet, though all the love possible for saints and angels to show falls, and will always fall, infinitely short of the Saviour's due, still it is a blessed privilege to love him at all, though in such a faint manner and in such a low degree. They that love him at all, wish to love him more. And more and more they shall love him through the ages of endless duration in heaven where they shall be like him, and see him as he is.

- How has reading the Song of Songs inspired your longing for Christ? Is there a next step you need to take?

Sources

Introduction. C. H. Spurgeon, 'A Bundle of Myrrh,' Sermon 558, in *The Most Holy Place: Sermons on the Song of Solomon* (Christian Focus, 1996), p. 103; and adapted from William of St. Thierry in Richard A. Norris (trans. & ed.), *The Song of Songs: Interpreted by Early and Medieval Commentators* (Eerdmans, 2003), pp. 10-11. © 2003. Wm. B. Eerdmans Publishing Company, Grand Rapids, MI. Reprinted by permission of the publisher; all rights reserved.

1. Gregory the Great, *On the Song of Songs*, trans. Mark DelCogliano, Cistercian Studies No. 244 (Liturgical Press, 2012), §3-4, pp. 110-11. © 2012 by Order of Saint Benedict, Collegeville, Minnesota. Used with permission.

2. Richard Sibbes, 'The Spouse: Her Earnest Desire After Christ,' *Works* (Banner of Truth, 1983), Volume 2, pp. 200-01.

3. Teresa of Avila, *Minor Works of St. Teresa*, trans. Benedictines of Stanbrook (Benziger Brothers, 1913), pp. 120, 122, 145-146, 155-156.

4. Hudson Taylor, *Union and Communion: Thoughts on the Song of Solomon* (Morgan & Scott, 1914), pp. 9-12, 17.

5. Bernard of Clairvaux, *Life and Works of St Bernard Volume IV: Cantica Canticorum*, trans. Samuel J. Earles (John Hodges, 1896), pp. pp. 13-15.

6. Ralph Robinson, *Christ All in All* (John Rothwell, 1660), pp. 303-05.

7. Charles H. Spurgeon, 'Rejoicing and Remembering,' Sermon 2641 in *The Most Holy Place* (Christian Focus, 1996), pp. 24-25.

8. Gregory of Nyssa, *Homilies on the Song of Songs*, trans. Richard A. Norris (Society of Biblical Literature, 2012), pp. 53, 55. Reprinted by permission.

9. Nilus of Ancyra in Richard A. Norris (trans. & ed.), *The Song of Songs: Interpreted by Early and Medieval Commentators* (Eerdmans, 2003), pp. 57-58. © 2003. Wm. B. Eerdmans Publishing Company, Grand Rapids, MI. Reprinted by permission of the publisher; all rights reserved.

10. Alexander Moody Stuart, *The Song of Songs* (Wm. S. Rentoul, 1869), pp. 133-43.

11. Samuel Rutherford, Letter 41, *Letters of Samuel Rutherford: A Selection* (Banner of Truth, 1973), pp. 118-20.

12. Ralph Robinson, *Christ All in All* (John Rothwell, 1660), pp. 361-62, 365.

13. James Durham, *Clavis Cantici, or An Exposition of the Song of Solomon* (George Swintoun and James Glen, 1668), pp. 103, 107, 109.

14. George Burrowes, *Commentary on the Song of Solomon* (James S. Claxton, 1867), pp. 214-18.

15. Martin Luther, *The Letters of Martin Luther*, trans. Margaret A. Currie (Macmillan, 1908), pp. 5-6.

16. Charles H. Spurgeon, 'The Rose and the Lily,' Sermon 784, in *The Most Holy Place* (Christian Focus, 1996), pp. 128-29.

17. Thomas Boston, 'Sermon 13: Suitable Improvement of Christ the Apple Tree,' *Works*, ed. Samuel McMillan (George & Robert King, 1848), Volume 3, pp. 166-72.

18. Thomas Manton, 'Sermons on the Sacraments,' *Works* (James Nisbet & Co, 1873), Volume 15, pp. 363-64, 366-68.

19. Alexander Moody Stuart, *The Song of Songs* (Wm. S. Rentoul, 1869), pp. 173-75.

20. Matthew Henry, *An Exposition of the Old and New Testaments* (Barrington & Haswell, 1828), Volume 3, pp. 852-53.

21. Thomas Brooks, 'God's Delight in the Progress of the Upright,' *Works* (Banner of Truth, 1980), Vol. 6, pp. 349-51.

22. Robert Murray M'Cheyne, 'Sermon XXIV: The Voice of my Beloved,' *Memoir and Remains of R. M. M'Cheyne*, ed. Andrew A. Bonar (Banner of Truth, 1966), pp. 484-85.

23. Martin Luther, 'Treatise on Good Works,' trans. Johann

Michael Reu, public domain. https://www.gutenberg.org/files/418/418-h/418-h.htm. Accessed November 5, 2022.

24. Adapted from Gregory of Nyssa, *Homilies on the Song of Songs*, trans. Richard A. Norris (Society of Biblical Literature, 2012), pp. 163-69. Reprinted by permission.

25. Robert Murray M'Cheyne, 'Sermon XXIV: The Voice of my Beloved,' *Memoir and Remains of R. M. M'Cheyne*, ed. Andrew A. Bonar (Banner of Truth, 1966), p. 486.

26. Matthew Henry, *An Exposition of the Old and New Testaments* (Barrington & Haswell, 1828), Volume 3, p. 855.

27. Martin Luther, 'Concerning Christian Liberty,' in *First Principles of the Reformation: The Ninety-Five Theses and the Three Primary Works*, ed. Henry Wace & C. A. Buckheim (John Murray, 1883), pp. 111-13.

28. Alexander Moody Stuart, *The Song of Songs* (Wm. S. Rentoul, 1869), pp. 217-18.

29. Bernard of Clairvaux, *Life and Works of St Bernard Volume IV: Cantica Canticorum*, trans. Samuel J. Earles (John Hodges, 1896), pp. 456-58.

30. Charles H. Spurgeon, 'Darkness Before the Dawn,' Sermon 2478, in *The Most Holy Place* (Christian Focus, 1996), pp. 234-35, 237, 241.

31. Walter Hilton, *The Scale of Perfection* (Art & Book Company, 1908), pp. 282-84.

32. Bernard of Clairvaux, *Life and Works of St Bernard Volume IV: Cantica Canticorum*, trans. Samuel J. Earles (John Hodges, 1896), pp. 511-14.

33. James Durham, *Clavis Cantici, or An Exposition of the Song of Solomon* (George Swintoun and James Glen, 1668), pp. 160-62.

34. Charles H. Spurgeon, 'Love's Vigilance Rewarded,' Sermon 2485, in *The Most Holy Place* (Christian Focus, 1996), pp. 250-51.

35. Charles H. Spurgeon, 'The Real Presence: the Great Need of the Church,' Sermon 1035, in *The Most Holy Place* (Christian Focus, 1996), pp. 255-61.

36. George Swinnock, 'The Fading of the Flesh,' *Works* (James Nichol, 1868), Volume 3, pp. 460-61.

37. St Ambrose, 'Isaac, or the Soul,' §5.44-46 in Richard A. Norris (trans. & ed.), *The Song of Songs: Interpreted by Early and Medieval Commentators* (Eerdmans, 2003), pp. 149-50. © 2003. Wm. B. Eerdmans Publishing Company, Grand Rapids, MI. Reprinted by permission of the publisher; all rights reserved.

38. James Durham, *Clavis Cantici, or An Exposition of the Song of Solomon* (George Swintoun and James Glen, 1668), pp. 180-81.

39. Charles H. Spurgeon, 'Paved with Love,' Sermon 1134 and 'The Royal Pair in their Glorious Chariot,' Sermon 484, in *The Most Holy Place* (Christian Focus, 1996), pp. 281, 276-77, 289.

40. Alexander Moody Stuart, *The Song of Songs* (Wm. S. Rentoul, 1869), pp. 263-65.

41. Thomas Boston, 'Sermon 9: Christ's Invitation to his Bride,' *Works*, ed. Samuel McMillan (George & Robert King, 1848), Volume 3, pp. 118-19, 121-22, 124-25, 127-28.

42. Richard Sibbes, *Bowels Opened*, in *Works of Richard Sibbes*, ed. Alexander B. Grosart (Banner of Truth, 1983), Volume 2, pp. 23-25.

43. Matthew Henry, *An Exposition of the Old and New Testaments* (Barrington & Haswell, 1828), Volume 3, pp. 862-863.

44. Robert Murray M'Cheyne, 'Sermon VII: The Church a Garden and Fountain,' *Memoir and Remains of R. M. M'Cheyne*, ed. Andrew A. Bonar (Banner of Truth, 1966), pp. 378-80.

45. Charles H. Spurgeon, 'Christ's Estimate of his People,' Sermon 282, in *The Most Holy Place* (Christian Focus, 1996), pp. 296-301.

46. Richard of Saint Victor in Richard A. Norris (trans. & ed.), *The Song of Songs: Interpreted by Early and Medieval Commentators* (Eerdmans, 2003), p. 182. © 2003. Wm. B. Eerdmans Publishing Company, Grand Rapids, MI. Reprinted by permission of the publisher; all rights reserved.

47. J. C. Ryle, 'The Lord's Garden,' *The Upper Room* (Banner of Truth, 1970), pp. 231-42.

48. Charles H. Spurgeon, 'The Lord's Own view of his Church and People,' Sermon 1957, in *The Most Holy Place* (Christian Focus, 1996), pp. 314-18.

49. Honorius of Autun in Richard A. Norris (trans. & ed.), *The Song of Songs: Interpreted by Early and Medieval Commentators* (Eerdmans, 2003), pp. 183-84. © 2003. Wm. B. Eerdmans Publishing Company, Grand Rapids, MI. Reprinted by permission of the publisher; all rights reserved.

50. St John of the Cross, *A Spiritual Canticle of the Soul*, trans. David Lewis (Thomas Baker, 1909), pp. 137-39.

51. Richard Sibbes, *Bowels Opened*, in *Works of Richard Sibbes*, ed. Alexander B. Grosart (Banner of Truth, 1983), Volume 2, pp. 20-21.

52. Samuel Rutherford, Letter 41, *Letters of Samuel Rutherford: A Selection* (Banner of Truth, 1973), pp. 120-22.

53. Richard Sibbes, *Bowels Opened*, in *Works of Richard Sibbes*, ed. Alexander B. Grosart (Banner of Truth, 1983), Volume 2, Volume p. 70.

54. Robert Murray M'Cheyne, 'Sermon LIX: I Sleep, But My Heart Waketh,' (1837), *The Sermons of Robert Murray M'Cheyne* (Robert Carter, 1863), 341-42.

55. Charles H. Spurgeon, 'Nearer and Dearer,' Sermon 793, in *The Most Holy Place* (Christian Focus, 1996), pp. 379, 383-87.

56. Richard Sibbes, *Bowels Opened*, in *Works of Richard Sibbes*, ed. Alexander B. Grosart (Banner of Truth, 1983), Volume 2, pp. 114-17.

57. Charles H. Spurgeon, 'Nearer and Dearer, Sermon 793 and 'Heavenly Love-Sickness,' Sermon 539, in *The Most Holy Place* (Christian Focus, 1996), pp. 389-90, 393-94, 399-400.

58. Richard Sibbes, *Bowels Opened*, in *Works of Richard Sibbes*, ed. Alexander B. Grosart (Banner of Truth, 1983), Volume 2, p. 133.

59. John of Ford in Richard A. Norris (trans. & ed.), *The Song of Songs: Interpreted by Early and Medieval Commentators* (Eerdmans, 2003), pp. 213-14. © 2003. Wm. B. Eerdmans Publishing

Company, Grand Rapids, MI. Reprinted by permission of the publisher; all rights reserved.

60. Richard Sibbes, *Bowels Opened*, in *Works of Richard Sibbes*, ed. Alexander B. Grosart (Banner of Truth, 1983), Volume 2, pp. 153, 157-58.

61. Anne Dutton, *Hints of the Glory of Christ; as the Friend and Bridegroom of the Church from the Seven Last Verses of the Fifth Chapter of Solomon's Song in a Letter to a Friend* (J. Hart, 1748), pp. 35-37.

62. Anne Dutton, *Hints of the Glory of Christ; as the Friend and Bridegroom of the Church from the Seven Last Verses of the Fifth Chapter of Solomon's Song in a Letter to a Friend* (J. Hart, 1748), pp. 65-67.

63. John Owen, 'Communion with God,' *Works* (Banner of Truth, 1965), Volume 2, pp. 73-74.

64. James Durham, *Clavis Cantici, or An Exposition of the Song of Solomon* (George Swintoun and James Glen, 1668), pp. 313-14.

65. John Owen, 'Communion with God,' *Works* (Banner of Truth, 1965), Volume 2, pp. 77-78.

66. Anne Dutton, *Hints of the Glory of Christ; as the Friend and Bridegroom of the Church from the Seven Last Verses of the Fifth Chapter of Solomon's Song in a Letter to a Friend* (J. Hart, 1748), pp. 95-98.

67. John Flavel, 'The Method of Grace: Sermon XII,' *Works* (Banner of Truth, 1968), Volume 2, pp. 218-19.

68. Richard Sibbes, *Bowels Opened*, in *Works of Richard Sibbes*, ed. Alexander B. Grosart (Banner of Truth, 1983), Volume 2, pp. 168-70.

69. Gregory of Nyssa, *Homilies on the Song of Songs*, trans. Richard A. Norris (Society of Biblical Literature, 2012), p. 467. Reprinted by permission.

70. Richard Sibbes, *Bowels Opened*, in *Works of Richard Sibbes*, ed. Alexander B. Grosart (Banner of Truth, 1983), Volume 2, pp. 173-74, 188, 193.

71. Charles H. Spurgeon, 'The Church as She Should Be,' Sermon 984, in *The Most Holy Place* (Christian Focus, 1996), pp. 464, 472-75.

72. James Durham, *Clavis Cantici, or An Exposition of the Song of Solomon* (George Swintoun and James Glen, 1668), pp. 355-57.

73. John Gill, *Exposition of the Book of Solomon's Song Commonly Called Canticles* (William Hill Collingbridge, 1854), pp. 245-46.

74. Matthew Henry, *An Exposition of the Old and New Testaments* (Barrington & Haswell, 1828), Volume 3, pp. 872-73.

75. George Burrowes, *Commentary on the Song of Solomon* (James S. Claxton, 1867), pp. 394-400.

76. Madame Guyon, *The Song of Songs of Solomon*, trans. James W. Metcalf (A. W. Dennett, 1879), pp. 109-13.

77. Richard Sibbes, *Bowels Opened*, in *Works of Richard Sibbes*, ed. Alexander B. Grosart (Banner of Truth, 1983), Volume 2, pp. 58-59.

78. Charles H. Spurgeon, 'Good Works in Good Company,' Sermon 605, in *The Most Holy Place* (Christian Focus, 1996), pp. 527-31.

79. George Burrowes, *Commentary on the Song of Solomon* (James S. Claxton, 1867), pp. 425-26.

80. Samuel Rutherford, Letter 41, *Letters of Samuel Rutherford: A Selection* (Banner of Truth, 1973), pp. 122-23.

81. James Durham, *Clavis Cantici, or An Exposition of the Song of Solomon* (George Swintoun and James Glen, 1668), p. 430.

82. Thomas Boston, 'Believers a Mystery,' *Works*, ed. Samuel McMillan (George & Robert King, 1848), Volume 10, pp. 550-53, 557, 563, 577-78.

83. John Flavel, 'Sacramental Meditations: The Eleventh Meditation Upon Cant. vii.6,' *Works* (Banner of Truth, 1968), Volume 6, pp. 451-55.

84. Anne Dutton, *Hints of the Glory of Christ; as the Friend and Bridegroom of the Church from the Seven Last Verses of the Fifth*

Chapter of Solomon's Song in a Letter to a Friend (J. Hart, 1748), pp. 10-12

85. Charles H. Spurgeon, 'The Shulamite's Choice Prayer,' Sermon 364, in *The Most Holy Place* (Christian Focus, 1996), pp. 564-70.

86. John Gill, *Exposition of the Book of Solomon's Song Commonly Called Canticles* (William Hill Collingbridge, 1854), pp. 312-13.

87. James Durham, *Clavis Cantici, or An Exposition of the Song of Solomon* (George Swintoun and James Glen, 1668), pp. 462, 465-67.

88. Samuel Rutherford, Letter 40, *Letters of Samuel Rutherford: A Selection* (Banner of Truth, 1973), pp. 115-17.

89. Charles H. Spurgeon, 'The Bridegroom's Parting Word,' Sermon 1716, in *The Most Holy Place* (Christian Focus, 1996), pp. 586-89, 593, 596.

90. Augustus Toplady, 'A Sacramental Meditation on Cant. 8:14,' *The Works of Augustus Toplady* (Richard Baynes, 1825), Vol. 3, pp. 433-35.